What Is a Catholic?

PAUL H. HALLETT

WHAT IS

A CATHOLIC?

COLLIER BOOKS, New York, N.Y.

Collier–Macmillan Ltd., London

What Is a Catholic? originally appeared under the title
What Is Catholicity?

This Collier Books edition is published by arrangement
with The World Publishing Company.
Collier Books is a division of The Crowell-Collier
Publishing Company.

First Collier Books Edition 1961

Nihil obstat: George Curtis Tolman, C.M., *Censor*
Imprimatur: ✠ Urban J. Vehr, *Archbishop of Denver*
June, 24, 1955

Biblical quotations used herein are from the Douay translation.
Those of the New Testament are from the Confraternity of
Christian Doctrine edition.

Published simultaneously by Collier-
Macmillan Limited, London

Contents   5

Foreword

AN ATTEMPT to answer the question "What is Catholicity?" in a volume of somewhat over 250 pages would seem, at first thought, at least a moral impossibility. Though one could set down the essential basis of the Church in a sentence or a paragraph, even the ponderous *Catholic Encyclopedia* refuses to answer all the queries.

But Paul H. Hallett of the *Register* has provided us with the most comprehensive explanation of Catholic doctrine and life that I, for one, have ever seen between two rather close covers. And, what is more, the author, who is a convert, has perfused his treatment with much of the spirit of Mother Church and, incidentally, his deep love for her. The writer marches through his pages a jealous defender of Christ's truth, albeit a patient clarifier of the objections that might be made against her.

From his exhaustive definition of the term "catholicity" to his analysis of the Church-State question, Mr. Hallett omits nothing of real importance about his subject. Some points are, of necessity, skimmed through hurriedly, but nothing vital is missing.

One of the most interesting sections I found was that expounding the principles of Scholastic philosophy. The author shows, by principle and example, that Thomism, on which Catholic theological study is based, is "the philosophy of the common man." He proves that the Church's dialectic mirrors the way a man naturally acts and reasons—a Godsend in this day of mixed-up, subjective thinking.

Mr. Hallett's discussion of Church authority is an apologetical gem. Scripture and tradition, the Trinity and the angels, grace and the Incarnation are coherently presented in the dry light of reason and history, but find warmth in their human application.

The section dealing with the moral law leaves little to the reader's imagination, either as to basis or as to practical obligation. Mathematical precision marks the statement of principles and their force.

In the chapters on the Church Sanctifying, the author makes real to the reader the life line of divine grace given His Church by the Master. Penance, or Confession, particularly is shown to be not the stumbling block that many non-

Catholics believe it to be; rather is it shown to be a psychological as well as a spiritual aid to salvation.

The treatment of the Church progressing brings up many interesting points on the evolution of Church dogma. And not a few non-Catholics will be startled to learn how tolerant the "intolerant" Catholic Church can be—in the right spheres.

The author-editor concludes his study with a remarkably cogent discussion of "principle and policy." He explains, with striking examples, that one who is inclined to oppose the Church must do so on principle, and cannot logically rail at her for forming her policy according to the principles Christ gave her.

From Aristotle to Newman, from the ancient Latin Fathers to modern theologians (even Protestant), quotations fall into line to highlight the great structure of Catholic faith.

Another aspect of *What Is Catholicity?* that is enlightening to Catholic and non-Catholic alike is the insertion of chapter after chapter on modern religious problems, moral and otherwise. Such points are expounded, each in its place, as, the authority to educate, evolution, progress in moral science, the relation of Church to civil law, the salvation of non-Catholics, the morality of war, the welfare state, sex education, divorce, and the world state.

The author's theme, beautifully recurrent, is that the Church is for all men and regulates every phase of human life. The reader, though he may have to draw upon his reserves of knowledge in the reading, will find that the Catholic Church is now a more familiar, more reasonable, and more lovable entity than he had perhaps dreamed of before.

REV. ROBERT KEKEISEN
ASSOCIATE EDITOR,
The Register

March 23, 1955

What Is a Catholic?

Introduction

IN THE LAST ANALYSIS, there are but two great classifications in the religious world, Catholic and non-Catholic. There is one religion that speaks with authority, set over against others that do not. One religion has domiciled itself everywhere on earth. One world religion teaches a doctrine and enforces a discipline that are everywhere the same in essence. Just one religious society claims to be founded by a God-Man and to exist as inseparably with Him as the trunk of a body exists with its head.

Just this religious body claims to be necessary for the eternal happiness of every man beyond the grave, so that no man can be saved unless he is either a member of the Church or one who has the intention or desire of entering this society. This desire may be implicit, i.e., if I knew the Church to be true I would join it.

All history prior to about 29 A.D., when the Divine Spirit possessed the disciples of Christ at Pentecost, cannot be understood without reference to that event; and man's spiritual pilgrimage in all succeeding time will follow the fortunes of the Catholic Church until this planet has run its course and all men stand before the Throne.

One-fifth of the human race is Catholic—the largest religious grouping in history. Yet the Catholic Church is so true to its name that it is not content with making laws for its own members but embraces in its charity and missionary zeal every individual on earth. It claims to have jurisdiction, at least indirectly and in some cases, over people who may not know of its existence, or at least never suspect the truth of its claims, namely non-Catholics who are baptized. Even the unbaptized must submit in some things to her law; even they must submit to her terms if they marry Catholics.

But Catholicity overflows the boundaries of the world and embraces domains beyond sense. It is the only religion that teaches that all who achieve the end for which they were created belong in some sort to it, are saved only in reference to it, and on the strength of the favor its sacrifices and merits and prayers call down from God. In this world of the unseen there is the Church Suffering, composed of all the souls, of whatever religion they had on earth, who died in the mercy of God and are now expiating the punishment of their sins in

13

preparation for heaven. Culminating all is the Church Triumphant, in which are all the souls, likewise from every religion, who now rest in the blessed vision of God. All these are Catholics, though on earth they may have misconceived or felt bitterly about the Church Militant, the Church struggling on earth, the Catholic Church. All men on earth who fulfill God's plan are destined to be Catholics.

What other religion, be it ever so intolerant or fanatic, has ever made such sweeping claims, and made them so confidently and so serenely? What other religion on earth has anything like the Magisterium, that living voice that speaks with the same calm authority today as it did in the days of Clement, the fourth Bishop of Rome? What other teaching office on earth has ever presumed, as has this Magisterium of the Catholic Church, to settle definitively and for all time question after question about the only things in the world that ultimately matter? What other power claims to be the final arbiter on all questions of faith and morals? There is just one Man in history who has spoken with the voice of both man and God. There is only one society in all the centuries that has asserted its right to rule, give judgment, and make laws with the same authority as that Man.

This claim is so universal and imperious, and the body of doctrine that supports it so solid and consistent, that this Catholic religion has left a broad line of cleavage over the religious world, so that even the most divergent non-Catholic religious groups, when compared to the Catholic Church, seem to be on one side, and she on the other.

All this explains the special position that a Catholic must necessarily occupy in any symposium of religious views. In that species of religious literature that has grown up in recent years, wherein representatives of various denominations explain the tenets of their faith ("What Is a Protestant?" "What Is a Jew?" "What Is a Catholic?"), it is not the primary aim of these people to make converts but to give an authoritative statement of what is and what is not held by the group for which they speak. Neither shall it be my aim to plead the cause of the Church directly.

But there is this about Catholicity that is not true of any non-Catholic denomination. It is subjected continually to attack from some quarter or another. Misunderstandings there may be about Baptists, Lutherans, Presbyterians, Eastern Orthodox, Mormons, and Jews. Enemies they may also have, especially in the case of the last two groups. But as a rule no one is too much concerned about the teachings or disciplines of any of these religious divisions. It is only the Catholic

Church, whose presence is so immediately felt in the pronouncements of its Pope and Bishops, which so often touch the thought and conduct of millions outside the fold; in its strict marriage code, which indirectly affects so many people outside the Church; in the consistency with which it carries out its unyielding ethics in its hospitals; in the separate education of its youth—because of this, and deeper reasons, it is only the Catholic Church that is the object of widespread and inveterate hostility and of a misunderstanding that runs deep through generation after generation.

If the Catholic Church did not uphold her unique position she would not incur this enmity and misunderstanding; but then she would not be the Catholic Church. It is of the essence of anything Catholic both to attract and to challenge. Therefore one who would explain her cannot be indifferent and detached but must be in some degree an apologist.

As one who has been for sixteen years on the staff of the *Register,* in Denver, Colorado, the largest Catholic—indeed, the largest religious—newspaper in the world, and who has read hundreds of letters critical of Catholicity, I feel that simple ignorance about the Church is not too widespread today. We get the type of letter that asks, apparently in all sincerity, whether it is true that the Cardinal's hat that hangs in a certain Cathedral has been dyed with infants' blood. But such tales are no worry to the Catholic newspaperman.

In the same mail that brought the letter about the infants' blood came another, written by a woman of some attainments, who asked why, since the Pope obviously had changed the centuries-old law of the Church regulating the Communion fast, he could not give her a dispensation from her invalid marriage, so that she could again frequent Communion.

This woman failed to make the distinction that law is not just law, but is both human and divine. Human laws as well as divine are registered in the code of the Church, and what men—even Churchmen—have made, men may take away. But the Church is powerless to change or dispense in the divine law governing the indissolubility of Christian marriage. All the murmurs, which plague a Catholic Ask-Learn writer's existence immediately after a celebrity is married in the Church, after procuring a civil divorce from an invalid marriage, need not have arisen if the murmurers had known or reflected on the teaching of the Church regarding her right as the Spouse of Christ to lay down impediments to marriage, or the necessity she has of upholding the divine law.

Another fruitful source of misunderstanding about the Church is the attempt to judge her, not by *her* principles, but by those of her critics. When this reaches an extreme form it is bigotry.

When, for example, Paul Blanshard calls the Catholic marriage laws *superfluous,* because the state has its own set of statutes governing marriage, he is trying to make his principle, that the state is the supreme arbiter of marriage, the test of the rightness or wrongness of religious bodies that conceive Matrimony as essentially above legislative fiat. The thing that Blanshard should have done, and which he has never done, was to attack the Church in her divine claims, the roots of her authority. The same complaint may be made against those who, though claiming complete loyalty to religious freedom, would implicitly deny the right of religious education by denying all benefits of the commonwealth to the child in the parochial school.

Four-fifths of the opposition to the Church would disappear if those who mistrust her would ask themselves: Why does she act like this? Are the principles on which she acts sound? Do her claims make a valid and forcible brief in the court of reason and history? Even by the pragmatic test, so dear to many Americans, has she shown her power?

Cardinal John Henry Newman, in his *Present Position of Catholics in England* (p. 294f), made a classic plea for this necessity of understanding the principles of Catholicity:

"Why may not my First Principles contest the prize with yours? They have been longer in the world; they have lasted longer, they have done harder work, they have seen rougher service . . .

"Take your First Principles, of which you are so proud, into the crowded streets of our cities . . . try to work society by them. You think you can; I say you cannot . . .

"My principles, which I believe to be eternal, have at least lasted eighteen hundred years; let yours live as many months. That man can sin, that he has duties, that the Divine Being hears prayer, that He gives His favours through visible ordinances, that He is really present in the midst of them, these principles have been the life of nations; they have shown they could be carried out; let any single nation carry out yours, and you will have better claim to speak contemptuously of Catholic rites, of Catholic devotions, of Catholic belief."

The modern critic of the Church is constantly confusing Catholic moral doctrine with what is simply Catholic discipline. He speaks vaguely of "Vatican policies" when he should be speaking of Catholic dogmas. And yet there is little excuse for such confusion, for the Catholic system is clear and coherent and always has a reason for all that it demands. It is to explain the principles that guide Catholicity and interlace its doctrine, worship, and discipline that I have written this book. I have translated some dozen volumes of textbooks of moral and dogmatic theology, which form the staple of the education of every priest. These contain most of the principles that guide the priest in his work of teaching and guiding the people committed to his care.

To give a compendium of all the dogmatic utterances, the dogmatic and moral theology, the philosophy, the history, the constitution and government, the worship and devotions of the Catholic Church is a task that has so far bested the best of many-volumed encyclopedias. Obviously this is not my purpose. Neither am I concerned with answering even the objections and difficulties that are most commonly lodged against the Faith. What I propose to do is to give some idea of the nature of the Church, why she must act as she does and in what things she is free, the sources from which she elaborates her dogmas, the philosophy that supports her theology, the teaching office that guides the faithful. In pursuing this plan I have followed closely Catholic texts on philosophy, moral theology, and dogmatic theology that are used in seminaries for the education of priests.

Most people, including Catholics, never heard of Herve, Tanquerey, Noldin, Sabetti-Barrett, Arregui and Pruemmer, or Farges and Barbadette. Not too many have even a clear idea of what was taught by St. Thomas Aquinas, the source from which most of them draw. Yet these texts are used in the seminaries and mold the minds of future priests. These priests influence hundreds of millions every day, including non-Catholics. In the close-knit coherence of these texts the structure of Catholic thought emerges.

Chapter 1

What Is Catholicity?

THE CATHOLIC CHURCH does not, at first sight, have the most pretentious name in religion. Broadly speaking, *catholic* means "universal." Nor, of the four marks of the Church: Catholicity, holiness, unity, and Apostolicity, is the catholicity in all respects the greatest. But it will not take long to discover why the name *catholic* came to attach to the normative religion of the world, and why all other denominations envy it its title.

Catholic comes from two Greek combinations: *kath-olou,* meaning "everywhere, universally," and *kath-olon,* "according to, or with reference to, the whole." Note the word *holon,* meaning "the whole." This at once distinguishes both the man of *catholic* tastes and interests and the man who is a Catholic. No one who is either of catholic taste or of the Catholic religion can consistently be provincial or narrow; his mind will rise to an appreciation of peoples and cultures not his own. He orders his life and makes his judgments with reference to a whole that gives meaning and order to the world.

Here are some of the meanings the *Oxford English Dictionary* gives to *catholic*: (1) *Universal:* "Science is truly *catholic* and is bounded only by the universe." (2) *Touching the needs, interests, or sympathies of all men.* Thus *catholic* poetry is that which is good in all ages. (3) *Opposed to national:* "What was of *catholic* rather than national interest." (4) *Having sympathies with, or embracing, all sorts of men, their feelings, tastes, etc.:* "Of these two universities, Cambridge is decidedly the most *catholic* (not Roman catholic but human catholic)." (5) *Quality of being comprehensive in feeling, taste, sympathy, etc.; freedom from sectarian exclusiveness or narrowness.*

I have gone to this length in giving these common meanings of the word *catholic* because I want to emphasize the fact that every one of them must belong also to Catholic as the designation of a religious body. Everything that is included under the anme of catholic must also be embraced by the Catholic spirit; else it would forfeit one of its most distinctive claims, which is catholicity, the quality of appealing to minds in all ages and lands.

Catholicity is a word that follows the fortunes of the adjective *catholic,* both upper and lower case. The *Oxford English Dictionary* gives its common meaning as "the quality of being comprehensive in feeling, taste, sympathy, etc.; freedom from sectarian exclusiveness or narrowness." Applied as a proper noun, it has two meanings: (1) "Of a Church or doctrine, the character of being universally recognized or diffused." It is in this sense that the word catholicity is used by Catholics as one of the four marks distinguishing their Church. (2) "The character of belonging to, or being in accordance with, the Catholic Church . . . specifically, of the Church of Rome: The doctrine of faith of the Church; Catholicism."

At every point Catholicity agrees with catholicity. This liberality of taste and sentiment, this broadness of sympathy, this universality of interest are nowhere better exemplified than in the amazing career of Pope Pius XII. I have before me a Spanish magazine that advertises the latest collection of his encyclicals and allocutions; they number 220, and keep increasing from week to week. In 1954 he delivered about fifty-four discourses and radio messages, from canonization sermons to addresses to international congresses on many subjects. He wrote four encyclicals to the universal Church. In 1953 his important messages numbered over eighty.

In one fortnight (September 23–October 6, 1954), Pius addressed, and addressed intelligently, a delegation of the tenth assembly of the International Geodetic and Geophysic Union, an international congress of the metallurgical industry, representatives of the linen and hemp manufactories, and the Fifth International Congress of Ceramics. Innumerable in his period of office as successor to Peter have been his allocutions to representatives of such varied interests and occupations as beekeeping, tramway conducting, tourist agencies, athletic associations, scientific conventions, medical conventions, learned societies—to say nothing of his addresses to envoys to the Holy See and to religious orders and societies.

In all these talks the word *catholic—kath-olon,* with reference to the whole—comes out in all its richness of meaning. In the four addresses I mentioned Pius opened his discourse, as he always does, with a review of the history and achievements of the profession or business he was talking about. There was no perfunctory saying of "a few words," but a talk that men engaged in casting iron, or molding clay, or making garments could understand and appreciate.

But all these addresses had one thing in common—they all centered about one unified view, the dignity of vocation in the service of God.

The ironmasters the Pope warned not to put their selfish interests above all, but to have at heart the temporal and spiritual needs of their workers. To the hemp and linen industrialists he presented an affecting picture of the part that linen played in the garments of the priests under the Mosaic Law; how it supplied the material for Christ's burial shroud; how it now is woven into the vestments the priest wears while saying Mass. Before the representatives of the ceramics industry he drew a mind-picture of clay being molded under the potter's hand, and he compared this with man's formation by his Creator. From this he took occasion to remind his listeners that the vase is independent of the potter, once it leaves his wheel, but man is always under the power of his Creator, whose sustaining action he needs at every moment of his existence.

Thus the Pope is catholic, and must be catholic, because he

must see everything in the world, including things that have but a remote relation to doctrine and worship, under the aspect of an eternal whole. There is nothing in the world that could not conceivably have some interest for a Catholic, simply as a Catholic. He, more than any other man, could, if consistent with his religion, make his own that famous line of Terence: *Homo sum, humani nihil a me alienum puto,* I am a man, and nothing that concerns man do I deem outside my concerns.

For example, the *Register,* most widely circulated Catholic newspaper, which keeps scrupulously clear of politics or anything not connected in some way with Catholicity, has dealt with thousands of questions in history, philosophy, science, industry, and government, which at first sight might seem to have no relation to the purposes of a Catholic newspaper, but all of which fit naturally into the edifice of Catholic doctrine. This universality of interests and concerns that marks the Catholic Church is important to bear in mind when we discuss the frequent objection brought against her; namely, that she "interferes" with medicine, politics, or the private lives of the people.

The word *Catholic,* in the religious sense, was first introduced to the world by an Eastern Bishop making his way to the center of the world under armed escort, there to be ground by the jaws of beasts in the Roman arena. Recurring to his frequent theme "Obey the Bishops!" St. Ignatius of Antioch exhorted the Smyrneans (*Epistle to the Smyrneans,* viii): "Wherever the Bishop appears, let the congregation be present; just as wherever Jesus Christ is, there is the Catholic Church."

Here St. Ignatius, who wrote in the year 107, not long after the death of the last of the Apostles, may be using the word "Catholic" to designate the universal Church, in opposition to particular churches in the various cities. But the emphasis on unity of doctrine that runs through his seven epistles shows that he had in mind the universal Church that maintains pure doctrine. At the beginning of the third century the word was used in precisely the same sense as it is today, to designate the True Church, in opposition to schisms or heretical sects.

Early in the history of Christian literature writers were struck by the wonder of a Church that had spread everywhere within the known world and had nevertheless retained its unity. The philosopher Justin, who died about the year 165, notes in his *Dialogue with Trypho* (cxvii): "There is not one single race of men, whether barbarians, or Greeks, or whatever they may be called . . . among whom prayers and giving of thanks [the sacrament of the Eucharist, the Mass] are not offered through the name of the crucified Jesus."

A generation later, toward the end of the second century, St. Irenaeus, Bishop of Lyons, gave the classic expression to Catholicity in these words, which begin the tenth book of his monumental work against the Gnostic heretics:

"The Church, though scattered through the whole world to the ends of the earth, received from the Apostles . . . this teaching and this faith. . . . This faith the Church carefully guards, as though it dwelt in a single house; this doctrine it believes as though it had one soul and heart; this creed it teaches and transmits as if it possessed one mouth.

"For, although there are many different languages in the world, there is one and the same power of tradition. The churches founded in Germany teach no different doctrine from those in Ireland or the surrounding Celtic countries; those in the East, or those in Egypt, do not differ from those in North Africa. Just as the sun, the creature of God, is one and the same in the whole world, so also is the preaching of the truth, the light that shines everywhere and illumines all men who wish to come to a knowledge of the truth. Neither is different doctrine taught by more cultured and able among these leading churches, nor is tradition diminished by those who are weak in controversy. For, since there is one and the same faith, it is neither added to by the effective speaker nor diminished by the one less skilled." (Irenaeus, *Against Heresies,* i, 10, 2)

Here you have the essence of Catholicity, as it exists today and in all ages: a universality pervading nations, languages, races, thought processes, backgrounds, and cultures. This note of Catholicity, one of the four principal notes of the Church to which Catholic apologists appeal in support of her claims, is territorial, because everywhere men live they are followed by the yearning of the Church to bring in members for Christ. No other religion has come near to the Catholic in missionary ambition.

But Catholicity is above all human, because it claims to embrace every race; it yearns not so much for square miles to conquer as for wills and intelligences to bring under the law of Christ.

A little more than a century after Irenaeus wrote, St. Cyril of Jerusalem (315–386), the Bishop of that city, extended the word Catholic to even richer meanings. He writes in his *Catechesis* (xviii, 23), a manual of instruction for those preparing to be Christians:

The Church is called "Catholic, because it is diffused

throughout the world from one end to another [this is geographic catholicity, catholicity in its most proper sense]; and because it teaches universally and unfailingly everything that can come to the knowledge of men [catholicity of doctrine, properly called unity]; and also because every race of men is subject to right worship—princes and citizens, the educated and the ignorant [catholicity of persons, again catholicity in its proper meaning]; and finally because it cures and heals every kind of sin, and possesses every kind of virtue, by whatever name it may be signified, in deeds and words and spiritual gifts of every kind" [this might be called catholicity of virtue, or holiness].

When the Vatican Council of 1870 declared that the Church was by herself, namely by her wonderful sanctity and inexhaustible fruitfulness in all good things, and by her Catholic unity and unshaken stability, a great and standing motive of belief in her claims and an irrefutable witness of her divine mission, it repeated substantially the language of this fourth-century Bishop of Jerusalem.

St. Augustine (354–430) is a brilliant witness of how the men of early Christendom saw the Church as a standing miracle. In his explanation of Psalm lvi he remarked: "We are Catholics in every land, because we communicate with every land, wherever the glory of Christ has spread . . . O heretical madness! . . . You believe with me that Christ was exalted above the heavens, though we cannot see this, and you deny His glory above every land, which we do see."

Thus for the early Christian writers the Church was an extension of Christ, and the name Catholic indicated the diffusion throughout the known world of the orthodox Christian community, in contrast with other denominations, which were out of the main stream of Catholicity. Even the pagans, who made no scientific study of Christian beliefs, recognized that there was, besides the numerous sects that sprang up on the borderlands of Christianity during the first five centuries, a "Great Church," which was not the sum of all the groups calling themselves Christian, and which stood apart from them.

From ancient times to this, no other division of Christianity has been able to make the name *Catholic* stick. In his *Contra Epistolam Quam Vocant Fundamenti*, iv, St. Augustine of the fourth century declares: "Although all heretics wish to be styled Catholic, yet if anyone ask where is the Catholic place of worship none of them would venture to point out his own conventicle."

We find the same posture of mind today. There have been at some time or other perhaps a dozen sects that have prefixed the title of Catholic to their names. In Chicago, in the summer of 1954, there even took place a "Congress of Catholic Churches." The qualifier "Roman" is religiously fixed to the Catholic name by most non-Catholics when they are writing self-consciously—yet the Holy Catholic Apostolic Roman Church (the full title given it by the Vatican Council) is not felt to be a species under the genus "Catholic," as Presbyterianism is a species of Protestantism. The very name of Catholic, the very instancy of the Church in the world, precludes such a thought. In informal or unguarded moments, the simple word "Catholic" will always be used.

Catholicity is unique, first in point of numbers, since it includes 472,000,000 adherents. This is more than the combined total of 196,592,520 Protestants and 128,280,414 members of the Eastern Schismatic Churches. (*Britannica Book of the Year, 1953*) The figures for the Catholic population of the world are drawn from a study made by Father Adrien Bouffard, an expert in missionary statistics. (Reported in the *Register,* July 4, 1954.) The number of people who are Catholics also exceeds the number of those who are Mohammedans, or Taoists, or Buddhists, or any other clearly defined religion.

As a matter of fact, there is no country or region in the world in which the Catholic religion is not found. *Herder-Korrespondenz,* January, 1955, *Soziographische Beilage* No. 1 lists 112 regions of the world according to Catholic population, thirty-six of which have a Catholic majority. In 111th place stands morose and remote Mohammedan Afghanistan, where no Christian missionaries are allowed. Yet even Afghanistan has one thousand Catholics. Only Mongolia is listed as having none, but it is a fact that that long Red-ridden land has a Bishop, though he is in prison, imprisoned priests, and but lately banished or imprisoned nuns.

The expansion of Catholicity has kept pace with every geographical advance of the normative civilization of the world, and in fact has preceded most of them.

To the Catholic religion alone belongs the glorious privilege of meeting the national and individual characteristics of mankind by becoming all things to all men, and yet never yielding an inch of ground in doctrine or moral code. The Catholic religion is held, for instance, by the African native, who may live so near to savagery that his Negro Bishop must issue pastoral letters warning him against association with those who practice ritual murder. Yet he is not infrequently of such exemplary personal life that missionaries may point him out as a model to the faithful of Europe and America.

In the United States the Catholic Church has taken the lead in ending segregation in areas where it was most firmly entrenched. Before the historic decision May 16, 1954, of the United States Supreme Court, which outlawed racial public schools, some five Southern Catholic dioceses had eliminated segregation in their schools.

As children south of the Mason and Dixon Line went back to school in 1954, almost all public-school children still went their separate ways—whites to their schools, Negroes to theirs. But in Catholic schools the list of States where white and Negro youngsters were sitting side by side reads like a roll call of a Southern political caucus.

In South Africa the Catholic Church is a Black Church, save only for a few thousands, and has been foremost in its resistance to the apartheid policy. Catholic nations, such as France and Brazil, have long been known for the singular absence of the color line.

More than any other missionary religion, the Catholic Church has taken native races into her priesthood and Hierarchy. The second Bishop of Portland, Maine, Augustine Healy, was the son of a mulatto mother, and born into slavery. Of the sixty-eight Negro, or part-Negro, Catholic priests ordained in the United States within a century, not one has had his services confined exclusively to one racial group.

There are today, in Catholic missionary districts, fifty-seven Bishops, or men of Episcopal rank, of African or Asiatic race, not counting the Chinese Bishops, who in 1950, before the Red purge had done all its work, numbered twenty-five. The Hierarchy of Japan has long been solidly Japanese. In 1950 the number of Bishops of African or Asiatic race was forty-two (not including the Chinese). As fast as it is possible, wherever the Church penetrates, native converts become her Bishops and priests. The *kath-olou,* the *everywhere* in Catholicity, is an instinct pervading Catholic history, being first implanted by the words of the Master, who commanded His disciples to preach the Gospel to all men. (Matt. xxiv, 14)

As I indicated before, catholicity is a word normally used by the Church's theologians, not to designate the entire Catholic structure, but rather as one of the four marks by which it can be known that the Catholic Church is the one established by Christ. The three other notes follow:

1. Unity in the Catholic Church means the subordination of all the faithful to the same spiritual jurisdiction and the same teaching office. No one may make doctrine for himself; all Catholics must obey the laws enacted by the Church for their spiritual welfare. This unity implies the profession of

the same faith, participation in the same means of salvation, and submission to the same pastors, especially the sovereign Roman Pontiff.

This unity does not mean uniformity. No wider range of types exists on earth than is found among the people who bear the Catholic name. Catholic unity is confined to essentials, as determined by the Church. There is a wide area of free discussion; rites and religious customs vary pleasingly.

Submission to a common authority, however, is essential to any unity. This means that the Church of Christ can and must bind the consciences of her subjects.

2. Apostolicity can be defined as continuous succession from the time of the Apostles in the government of the Church. This means, according to the Baltimore Catechism, No. 3, that the Church was founded by Christ on the Apostles and that it has always been governed by their lawful successors, the Bishops, and that the sovereign power of St. Peter has been passed down through an unbroken line to the present occupant of the See of Rome. Being Apostolic, the Church must also be indefectible, that is, unable to teach doctrine at variance with that transmitted by the Apostles. (*Ibid.*, No. 159)

3. Sanctity, as a note of the Church, means that "the Catholic Church is holy because it was founded by Jesus Christ, who is all-holy, and because it teaches, according to the will of Christ, holy doctrines, and provides the means of leading a holy life, thereby giving holy members to every age." (*Ibid.*, Nos. 156, 157)

The Church is holy because it is preserved against error by the Holy Spirit. It cannot give countenance to anything fundamentally wrong, whether in doctrine or morals. It cannot demoralize any people, however strange, among whom its doctrine is preached and its discipline enforced. It must always raise the moral tone of every civilization that it pervades, and it has done so. What moral gain has there been—in the family, in the individual, in government—that was not indebted at least remotely to the doctrine it has expounded?

When the Church speaks of "holy members" it does not mean men and women of ordinary honesty. It has reference to superior virtue, existing as a permanent state in a good number of men, and not merely in some. It is a combination of superior, and even heroic, virtues, in a not inconsiderable minority of the Catholic body in every age, even the most critical, that constitutes the boast of the Church and explains the veneration in which the saints are held. If the Church could not produce saints it would not be the Church.

By "heroic virtue" nothing spectacular is necessarily meant. The term simply means that one performs virtuous acts (commonly the plain duties of one's state in life) with uncommon promptness, ease, and pleasure, all for the love of God and with complete control over natural inclinations.

The Church claims to be pre-eminent in the production of saints not only because of holy doctrine but because of its sacramental system, whereby it makes available the means of God's help that flows to men through Baptism, Holy Orders, Penance, Matrimony, Extreme Unction, Confirmation, and the Eucharist.

The "Holon" in Catholicity

"The Church," wrote Leo XIII, in his encyclical *Satis Cognitum* (June 29, 1896), "belongs not only in its origin but in its entire constitution to the genus of things accomplished by free intention. Therefore we must inquire, not how the Church can be one, but how her Founder willed her to be one." The Church is indeed of supernature, and not of nature. Yet Catholicity so harmonizes with human nature that it may be said that even a purely natural religion, so far as it was true, would have to approximate it.

St. Thomas More, in his *Utopia*, brought this out well. He imagined a people to exist outside the sphere of revelation but obedient to reason; and all Utopians gravitated to "that religion which seemeth by reason to surpass and excel the rest." The subjects of King Utopus had a religious organization and worship and discipline very like the Catholic. They had priests, who were expected to be holy and who were held in honor; they observed holy days, had sacrifices and sensuous religious ceremonies; they believed in miracles and had orders of men and women who embraced both the active and the contemplative life and practiced celibacy. King Utopus allowed freedom of worship but recognized "one religion which alone is trew."

In short, the Catholic religion answers man's craving for unity in diversity; it is the whole (*holon*) harmonizing all the parts. It contains doctrines of the widest divergency, all of which, however, fit so well into one another that the rejection of one almost necessitates the collapse of the whole edifice. When Luther affirmed that man is saved by faith alone he had to reject not only the authority of the Church that taught the efficacy of good works, but also the doctrine of indulgences, based upon good works, and those texts of Scripture—whole books, in fact—that uphold the merit of good works. This in turn led to doubt as to the inspiration of all Scripture.

In society, Catholicity, though teaching the essential equality of all men, emphasizes the need of subordination. In the family, according to the Catholic ideal, the father is king, the mother, queen, the children, subjects. In moral theology, there is a hierarchy of virtues. In philosophy, creation is conceived as so many steps—minerals, animals, human life, angels—leading up to God. The priesthood with its seven Orders—three major and four minor—is, in St. Thomas Aquinas' view, but a reflection of the hierarchy to be found in creation, whereby the lower are led to their end by the higher. This emphasis on gradations well explains how Catholic thought can be so lucid and rational. By viewing things as distinct, yet serving a higher thing, it avoids the confusions of pantheism.

The wholeness of Catholicity perfectly reconciles reason and mystery. There are mysteries in religion, because no finite mind can comprehend an infinite God. But, since reason as well as faith comes from God, reason can demonstrate a certain harmony between a mystery like the Incarnation of the Son of Man and man's needs. No small part of dogmatic theology is taken up with demonstrating that no mystery of faith involves a self-contradiction.

Because Catholicity is the religion that completely reconciles man with God, and since man was made for God, it follows that everything in the world that is good is in some sort Catholic. The use of temples dedicated to particular saints was admittedly influenced by the temples to various gods in pagan antiquity. Incense, lamps, and candles, votive offerings on recovery from illness, holy water, blessings of the fields, the marriage ring, images, ecclesiastical chant—all are of pagan origin, and sanctified by their adoption into the Church.

"So far," says John Henry Newman, "from her creed being of doubtful credit because it resembles foreign theologies, we even hold that one special way in which Providence has imparted divine knowledge to us has been by enabling her to draw and collect it together out of the world, and, in this sense, as in others, to 'suck the milk of the Gentiles and to suck the breast of kings.'" (*Development of Christian Doctrine*, p. 381)

Precisely because it was meant by God for all mankind, Catholicity is of all religions the least envious, though it is of all religions the most jealous. It is jealous as God is jealous, because it cannot temporize with anything contrary to its divine commission to teach and govern. But it is not envious, for envy is offended at another's good, and what good can there be outside the fold that cannot be brought into it?

Hence in a Catholic newspaper, and among Catholics generally, you will find little carping criticism of non-Catholic religionists, and often a generous admiration of some particular trait as being rightly a Catholic one.

This harmonization of human nature with God, which is a hallmark of Catholicity, also explains why it can and must be the most unbending of religions in all that must lead to God, and yet be entirely without fanaticism. The penances of some of the saints have been severe, but generally within reason, and under direction. Life in the religious orders is austere, but never eccentric.

Finally, for every religion that would be an unbroken whole there must be a center of cohesion—an authority. And if the whole is never to break it must be guaranteed in its judgments on faith and morals by a more than human power. To maintain Catholic doctrine always consistent there are the Bishops, and over the Bishops the Popes—Popes and Bishops the most divergent in virtue, character, age, and nationality, who must continue to be divergent until the end of time; and yet Popes and Bishops united to the Christian people, who in matters of faith and doctrine must never be deceived, though men are deceived so often; Popes who agree among themselves century after century, whereas a man is rarely in agreement with himself from morning to evening. A religion so whole as that of Catholicity must be divine.

Chapter 2

What Is the Church?

CATHOLIC THEOLOGIANS lead up to this question by demonstrating man's need for the Church. Once the need is demonstrated we get a fair idea of what the Church must be.

As early as the time of Origen, in the third century, Christian apologists used the argument that man needed an authoritative guide to live even a good life according to nature. Aristotle gave us that sublime definition of God as "Pure Act," but Aristotle did not worship that Pure Act or persuade others to worship Him. The teachings of the best philosophers were only for the few. Modern thought-forgers, with their positivism, materialism, and agnosticism, are even farther from God, and they have subverted natural ethics.

As Origen pointed out seventeen centuries ago, most men can devote only a small part of life to seeking truth. Moreover, natural reason in most men is too obscured by passion and indolence to serve as a trustworthy guide to conduct; besides, what authority does any man have to teach truth to other men?

All this was enforced upon me one day when I was walking to work at the *Register*. A friendly truck driver, working for the same Catholic paper, overhauled me and gave me a lift. He opened his conversation with a remark that startled me as much as was Rudyard Kipling when he heard a Yankee farmer correct him: " 'Twarn't Montaigne, 'twar Montesquoo."

"I remember reading somewhere in St. Augustine's *Confessions* where he said that everything he did came hard for him," he said in his drawling voice, and then went on to make note of things that have escaped the penetration of those who are so often called philosophers today.

I reflected that not too many truck drivers, including Catholic truck drivers, have read St. Augustine. But every good Catholic truck driver comes into contact with St. Augustine's wisdom frequently through the sermons he hears. It is one of the glories of the Catholic Church that Aristotle, the Fathers of the Church, St. Thomas—men of the most brilliant intellect —can be brought down to the intellect of the most lowly.

This power of the Catholic Church to bring within ready reach all that is necessary for the right ordering of life is made dramatic in an unforgettable prose picture by one Raymond Brucker, a French convert from Utopian Socialism in 1848:

Why the Human Race Needs the Church

"At that time all the human race—that which was, that which is, and that which shall be, gathered together on a great plain, and hither summoned all the philosophers, past, present, and future.

"And the Human Race spoke thus to the philosophers: 'I have read all your works—yes, all of them—and I must say that I am still dissatisfied and bewildered. I have read all your works, and, after reading and rereading them, I have found myself in the midst of mournful and frightening shadows. I know less than before. Therefore I have summoned you, that I may pose again the great problem that torments me, and to make three demands of you.

" 'I want a book, a little book, of 10 or 20 pages, which contains all the truth in elementary and wholly transparent form; a little book that can be put into the pocket, and which costs only a few cents; a little book that is equally within the reach of the thinker, the poet, and even the masses who live only the practical and material life. This is the book, this is the reading I want.'

"The philosophers looked at one another in amazement—and many began to slip away and hide.

"The Human Race continued: 'Not only do I want a little book, which contains all the truth in 10 pages and popularizes it universally in time and space; but I want someone one day to come and offer me the example of all the virtues that are taught in this little book. And I want that example to be easily imitated by man, woman, and child. Can you give me the book? Can you give me the example I want?'

"Three-quarters of the philosophers had already disappeared. The Human Race, who had noticed this, began to be sad at heart. And it said again: 'This is not all. Not only do I need a lesson; not only do I need a deathless example; I also need an immortal institution . . . to guarantee and perpetuate the lesson and the example, by keeping them eternally alive.'

"When the Human Race had ended these words it cast a glance at its philosophers; and they were gone.

"Then the Human Race, the poor Human Race, wept hot tears. And, while it was thus immersed in sorrow, there suddenly appeared, from some quarter or other, a form of a Man, clothed in a kind of blouse, who bore on His shoulders a kind of beam—a great piece of wood, all bloody. The beam was crossed by another piece of wood—one might call it a Cross. And the Man had all his beautiful hair covered with blood; the blood ran over His eyes; the blood flowed in great drops down His whole body. He looked at the poor Human Race—so sweetly, so tenderly!

"Then He came slowly forward—with what majesty! He came carrying the enormous beam. He said in His tender voice: 'Do you wish the truth? I carry it; do you want a little book, which in 10 pages contains all the truth and can be understood by everyone? Here, take this little book.' And on the first page the Human Race read: Catechism.

"The Man continued: 'You have asked Me, not only for a lesson, but also for a living example. Here, look at Me. I am your God, who became Man to offer you an eternal pattern and to lead you to happiness. Lastly, you have requested an institution: Take it. Here is the Church.'

"And the Human Race fell on its knees and adored Jesus Christ." (Gautier, *Portrait du XIXe siècle, t. II*, pp. 343–345, quoted in *Enciclopedia Apologetica*, pp. 488–489)

The manuals of philosophy and theology that the student

for the priesthood studies in the seminary are but expansions of the catechism, from which the Catholic child learns of the origin of the world and the human race, the destiny of man in this life and the next, the relations of man with God and the duties of man toward man. From it he learns to reason in the manner of Aristotle, and draws conclusions at which Aristotle never arrived. It leaves no one without an answer to the questions of most vital interest to mankind. Whence did it derive this power? From a Church that never grows old, but advances constantly in wisdom and experience; from a Church that speaks as authoritatively as the Son of God become Man.

The Church, in its own spiritual sphere, is a society as sovereign as is the state. The Church, like the state, contains subordinate societies, but it owns no jurisdiction above it. Whatever it needs to attain its supernatural end, which is the salvation of souls, is conferred on it by Christ. He gave the end; therefore He furnished all the means necessary to the end, namely universal power, independent of every will that is not of God, to teach, govern, and sanctify all men until the end of the world. (Matt. xxviii, 19; xvi, 18 ff.; John xx, 22–23) Since it operates by divine commission, the Church claims the right to preach everywhere and it denies the right of any civil authority to forbid or restrict its jurisdiction.

One who enters this kingdom of the Church subjects himself to a code of laws that are not mere rules, such as any subordinate society has the right to make to determine conditions of membership, but true laws, having in all respects at least as much power to coerce the conscience as have the laws of the state. He submits to officers having for matters within their competence as much authority to command obedience in conscience as have those of this nation. All this is by way of saying that the Catholic Church is a visible and a perfect society.

The Church has the same subjects as the state, but not in the same way. By the law of nature, the state has authority over its subjects. Its end is to lead them to temporal welfare and prosperity. By the positive will of God, the Church has full jurisdiction over its subjects with the purpose of leading them to an end that is beyond this world. It is impossible for conflicts of a fundamental nature to arise between the two societies, except through the fault of men, and there is always a way of reconciling such quarrels as may arise by the subordination of the inferior (civil) power to the spiritual.

The Church is a monarchical society inasmuch as it has one ruler, the Sovereign Pontiff, or Pope, whose see is the city of

Rome. It is a hierarchical society inasmuch as it is ruled, as respects the individual Catholic communities, by Bishops, who hold their authority directly from God. It is important to remember that the Bishops are by no means simple delegates of the Pope, though they may not lawfully hold office without his approval. The institution of the episcopacy is so essential to the Church that without it it could not be the Church of Christ.

The Church is, finally, an indefectible society, or one which can never perish as long as this earth lasts, and which cannot fail of its end. It cannot teach false doctrine or go astray in any of the matters that are essential to man's last end. The Church is not a philosophy; it is a revelation, a faith, and a life. It is an existent reality, which has its own life, its essential conception of the world and of men, its own system, its peculiar organization. More than any state, it is a living body, which grows and takes in nourishment, and throws off impurities, and has antibodies in its blood stream that kill the poisons that would sap its strength.

The Church, in sum, is the prolongation of the Incarnate Word.

How the Church Began

One of the titles of the Church is "the bride of Christ." Indeed, no institution was ever so closely joined to one man as the Church is with her Founder. Like Christ, she is both human and divine. She is intolerant and dogmatic where He was intolerant and dogmatic. Like Him, she has the universal mission to teach all men and guide them to their eternal destiny.

Buddha and Confucius had disciples; Christ alone *called* men to follow Him. Even so, the Church calls on all men to obey His word. The very word "Church," from the Greek noun *ekklesia,* is derived from the verb *kalein,* meaning "to call." The men whom the Master called went by the name of Apostles, which means "the sent," "the commissioned." They formed a privileged group, a little society to themselves, whom Jesus trained, not for their benefit only, but that they might be teachers of others. They were the seed of the Church.

When Christ warned this group about the obligation of correcting the brethren He told it: "If he [the erring one] refuse to hear them, appeal to the Church, but if he refuse to hear even the Church, let him be to thee as the heathen and the publican. Amen I say to you, whatever you bind on earth shall be bound also in heaven, and whatever you loose on earth shall be loosed also in heaven." (Matt. xviii, 17–18)

Here is the first mention of the word "Church" in the New Testament, a word that in Greek means "an assembly" and in the Old Testament was applied to the entire people of God. The Master intended the Church to be the new Israel, whose authority was to endure forever.

The God-Man was crucified and rose from the dead. His parting words as recorded at the end of the Gospel of Matthew are these: "Go, therefore, and make disciples of all nations, baptizing them in the name of the Father, and of the Son, and of the Holy Spirit, teaching them to observe all that I have commanded you; and behold, I am with you all days, even unto the consummation of the world." (Matt. xxviii, 19–20)

With the power Christ claimed in heaven and on earth, as the Son of God and as the Messias sent by God, He sent them to evangelize the world. He had given them power to govern; He now gave them the mission to teach. Through this preaching of the Word, and its acceptance by the nations, the Kingdom of God was to be established, developed, and perpetuated. The jurisdiction of the Apostles was limited to making God reign in men's hearts, but within those limits it was supreme.

The spiritual power of the Apostles had extended to loosing or binding the most intimate bonds of man, those in which the soul is directly related to God—I mean the bonds of conscience. "Whose sins you shall forgive," Jesus told the Apostles, "they are forgiven them, and whose sins you shall retain, they are retained." (John xx, 23)

In these words of this commission the distinctive marks of the Church already stand out: Man's relations with God are not left to the individual, but are under the control of authority. This authority was established by the will of God, and those who hold it are not all men, but only a few, namely the Apostles. And, since the Apostles would not live forever, this authority was to descend to successors.

This authority, within its own sphere, has no limits and is guaranteed against error or abuse by divine power. It is independent of the will of men. The successors of the Apostles in this divinely given authority are the Bishops.

But this Kingdom of God was to be not only a hierarchical society, ruled by Bishops, but also a monarchical society, with a head that was to rule both Bishops and people. He was called Peter and in Aramaic *Kepha*, "rock."

Nothing is more evident than the position of this man. Peter is the only one to speak in the name of the twelve. In the solemn events of His life, Jesus selected always a group of three, who were always the same, and the first of the three was always Peter.

When the time came for Christ to reveal His mission and character, He asked Peter to tell Him who He was. The Apostle replied: "Thou art Christ, the Son of the living God." The Master then addressed the disciple: "Blessed art thou, Simon, son of John, for flesh and blood has not revealed this to thee, but My Father in heaven. And I say to thee, thou art Peter (Kepha), and upon this rock I will build My Church, and the gates of hell shall not prevail against it. And I will give thee the keys of the kingdom of heaven; and whatever thou shalt bind on earth shall be bound in heaven, and whatever thou shalt loose on earth shall be loosed in heaven." (Matt. xvi, 16–20)

Peter could not have been the rock foundation on which the Church was to rest unless he enjoyed supreme power to teach and rule souls. This authority was promised in the words: "I will give to you the keys of the kingdom of heaven," and: "Whatever thou shalt bind on earth shall be bound in heaven."

In the Gospel of Luke, Christ prays for one man, Peter, though all were tempted by Satan. Peter was to strengthen the faith of those who would fail. (Luke xxii, 32)

After the crucified Christ had risen from the dead, the Master conferred on Peter the power that He had promised: "Feed My lambs," He said; "feed My sheep." (John xxi, 15–17) Among all writers of antiquity the word "feed" designated a social authority when used metaphorically. Here again, one individual was addressed, called by a personal name, "Simon, son of John"; and Christ demanded from him a strictly personal love—"dost thou love Me more than these do?" (John xxi, 15)

The Lord ascended into heaven. For some time the initial group of believers remained in Jerusalem, awaiting a tremendous event their Master said would take place. The Spirit came upon them in what Acts ii, 3, describes as "tongues like fire." The Church was born.

After Pentecost, the Apostles acted collectively as officers of the newly formed religious society. They exercised the threefold power of teaching, governing, and sanctifying. (Acts i, 12–26; ii, 37–43; iv, 35–37; v, 1–11; 28–41; viii, 14–20) Over both Jewish and Gentile converts their authority was accepted as divine, and which they often claimed in their epistles, whether in teaching (I Cor. ii, 1–5; vii), or in judging (I Cor. v), or in rebuking (I Cor. vi), or in making laws or giving precepts (I Cor. xi, xii, xiv).

Under the Apostles inferior ministers already began to appear, called deacons and presbyters and Bishops, who together with the Apostles formed a true Hierarchy. (I Pet. ii, 9, 12, 25; v)

Not all the presbyters or Bishops seem to have received the fullness of Apostolic authority. The title of Bishop seems in the beginning to have been another designation for the same minister, who was also called a presbyter. But some of these ministers received the fullness of the priesthood, together with authority to communicate this power to others. These alone, and not the presbyters of the second rank, were truly called the successors of the Apostles, whom today we call Bishops.

St. Paul conferred the fullness of the priesthood on Timothy and Titus, whom he sent to organize churches and to whom he committed the faculty of creating pastors and deacons by the laying on of hands (I Tim. iii, 1 ff.; v, 17–22; Tit. i, 5 ff.), and it is probable that he gave the same authority to other disciples.

St. John conferred the fullness of the priesthood on certain men, which included a jurisdiction that was reserved to the successors of the Apostles alone. (Apoc. i–iii) St. Ignatius, writing about the year 107, supposes in his epistles that the Episcopate had been instituted for some time. He asserted that there is one Bishop in every church, to whom the presbyters and deacons must be subject. We also have several lists of Bishops, which in various churches traced the Episcopal line down to the first century, or even to the Apostles.

From these and other facts we may infer that the Apostles committed the fullness of the priesthood to some of their disciples in order that they might govern individual churches. In the second century and later, these men were called Bishops, a word meaning literally "overseer."

Nowhere in the early Church is there any evidence of a democracy in the matter of teaching and transmitting Christian doctrine. The Apostles declared that the Holy Spirit was with them as a witness of all that they preached (Acts v, 32) and co-operated with them in framing both dogmatic and disciplinary decrees. (Acts xv, 28) And therefore they demanded the full assent of the intellect and anathematized anyone, even an angel, who should teach a different Gospel. (II Cor. x, 5)

In their writings the Apostles affirmed that the Church is the pillar and mainstay of the truth (I Tim. iii, 15) and that the doctrine they taught was a trust to be faithfully guarded and not to be confused with erroneous novelties. (I Tim. vi, 20–21)

The doctrine transmitted by the Bishop was a safe rule of faith from which no one was allowed to depart, as St. Ignatius wrote in his epistles to the Ephesians (iii, iv, v, vi, xvii), to the Trallians, to the Smyrneans, and to the Philadelphians. By the end of the second century, councils of Bishops were formed against heretics, and these were regarded as authentic organs of truth. The rule of Christian faith was a living, infallible teaching office, represented by the body of Bishops.

Over these Bishops was a head, who was first the Apostle Peter, who came to Rome and was Bishop of the city until the end of his life. In the first three centuries the pre-eminence of the Church of Rome was recognized by all Christians. Toward the end of the first century, some time between the years 93 and 97, the Roman church assumed the right and duty of obliging the Corinthians to heal the schism which had formed in that Christian community. The man who spoke in the name of that church, Clement, taught as one having authority. He was the third successor of Peter.

"You will give us joy and gladness," this Bishop of Rome writes to the Christians of Corinth, "if you are obedient to the things that we have written through the Holy Spirit, and root out the wicked passion of your jealousy according to the entreaty for peace and concord which we have made in this letter. And we have sent faithful and prudent men, who have lived among us without blame from youth to old age, and they shall be witnesses between you and us. We have done this that you may know that our whole care has been and is directed to your speedy attainment of peace." (*I Clement*, lxiii, Loeb translation)

Surely, these are the words of a man burdened with the care of the whole Church.

At the beginning of the second century, Ignatius, Bishop of Antioch, wrote to the Romans, "to the Church that presides in the place of the region of the Romans, a Church worthy in its holiness, which presides over the fellowship of love." To other Christian communities Ignatius indited letters urging them to submission to the Bishops and condemning heresies. Only in his epistle to the Romans is this language absent.

In the course of the second century, many came to Rome to visit the Bishop and to seek his decision on matters of faith and discipline. Such, for example, was Polycarp, a disciple of John; Abercius, Bishop of Jerusalem; and even heretics, such as Marcion and the Montanists.

Toward the end of the second century we find a notable witness to the Roman primacy in St. Irenaeus. St. Irenaeus declares that truth is found in the churches established by the

Apostles. But, since it would take too long to investigate the traditions of all the churches, it suffices to know those that are received in the Church of Rome, for this Church constitutes a rule of faith with which all the other churches must agree, on account of the spiritual pre-eminence that it holds from the Apostle Peter who founded it: "For with this church, because of its superior authority, the whole Church must agree, that is, all the faithful everywhere; for it is in this church that what was taught by the Apostles has been always preserved by those who are everywhere. . . ." (*Against Heresies,* iii, 3)

In the third century many, including Bishops from various provinces, had recourse to the Bishop of Rome, either to give an account of their faith or to settle controversies. In the fourth and fifth centuries, the primacy of the Church of Rome was asserted so clearly, in word and deed, that no doubt can be entertained of its existence.

In the fourth and fifth centuries we find, for example, St. Ambrose, Bishop of Milan, teaching that the Church of Rome is the head of the whole Catholic world and that the sign of true faith is communion with that Church. We see St. Augustine, the greatest intellectual luminary of his age, admitting appeals from his own judgment to the Holy See and acknowledging that the provincial councils derived their chief authority from the approval of the Sovereign Pontiff. St. Jerome writes to Pope Damasus: "I am joined in communion with Your Beatitude. On this rock I know the Church is built. Whoever shall eat the lamb outside this house is an outcast." (Rouet de Journel, *Enchiridion Patristicum,* 1346)

All the early Church councils admitted the sovereign authority of the Roman Pontiffs. In the Council of Ephesus, held in 431, St. Cyril appealed to the Roman Pontiff for a decision and definition. Pope Celestine chose Cyril as his representative to preside over the council. He also sent legates, one of whom, the Presbyter Philip, explicitly asserted before the members of the council, without a single protesting voice, the primacy of Peter and his successors, the Roman Pontiffs, over the universal Church.

In the Council of Chalcedon (451), the celebrated epistle of Pope Leo condemning the errors of Eutyches was read with the approbation of all the members. "Peter has spoken through Leo!" they cried.

This primacy of the Roman See was not created by the ambition of the Bishops of Rome, for all the Sovereign Pontiffs claimed this sovereign jurisdiction as a duty and a responsibility. "We carry the burden of all who are burdened," wrote Pope St. Siricius (384–398) to Bishop Himerius in 385—"nay rather, the Apostle Peter carries them in us." (Denziger, *Enchiridion Symbolorum,* pp. 42–43)

Neither can the Roman primacy be ascribed to the pre-eminence of Rome as a political center, for both the Roman Pontiffs and the other leaders of the early Church asserted that this position arose from the will of Christ, who made Peter and his successors the head of the universal Church.

This unique power of primate of the entire Christian community was not exercised so frequently in the beginning as it is now. Its presence was in the early centuries felt rather than asserted. Yet it was there, unmistakably. As far back as we have documents emanating from Rome, we find the calm assurance that the occupants of the chair of Peter are commissioned by Christ to rule the Church: "We carry the burdens of all who are burdened—nay rather, the Apostle Peter carries them in us."

Chapter 3

Between Reason and Faith: Thomism

CATHOLICITY is a religion of faith; its doctrines are derived from an *Ipse Dixit*—the word of God speaking directly to men. Nevertheless, it is a maxim of the Catholic schools that "faith hungers after understanding." Hence philosophy is essential to Catholicity. By philosophy we know truths in their highest causes, by the natural light of reason.

The Church teaches that reason can never contradict faith, and in fact reason is the means we must use to take the first necessary steps toward faith. Some things, like the existence of God the Rewarder and Creator, we know through both reason and divine revelation. Other things, like the Incarnation of the Son of God, we cannot know by reason but can understand better by the light of the analogies with which reason supplies us.

I have entitled this chapter "Between Reason and Faith," because in this order of the world the supernatural has so penetrated the natural that even non-Christians can never be viewed in the same light as the men from Mars, as mere rational animals. Even in the philosophy taught in the Catholic schools faith and reason interplay, faith fencing reason from pitfalls, reason deepening the meaning of faith.

In a book like Denziger's *Enchiridion Symbolorum*, a compendium of all the dogmatic pronouncements of Popes and Councils, you will find both assertions of reason's rights and powers and cautions about its limitations. The Church has both condemned attempts to explain the Christian mysteries and upheld the power of reason to know the existence of God and the immortality of the soul.

This interplay of faith and reason is found even in the catechism that is taught to small children. Here we find philosophy, as well as faith, on almost every page. The opening words of the Baltimore Catechism No. 3, after the question: "Who made us?" are: "Reason unaided by revelation can prove that God exists. It knows that this vast universe could not have come into being by its own powers. . . ." A little later, under the heading: "What is a spirit?" the philosophical reason for immortality is given as follows: "The soul of man is a spirit, which does not die because it is simple, having no integral parts, and because it is spiritual, that is, entirely independent of matter in its being and in its own proper acts." The Catholic child from the dawn of reason learns to think like Aristotle.

Catholicity is always a *reasoning*, or rather a *rational*, religion, even when it accepts things beyond man's natural powers to know. The philosophy that it employs in its work of safeguarding revealed truths is a catholic philosophy, that is, a philosophy that can be understood more or less by every man, woman, and child throughout the world. This catholic philosophy is called Thomism, after St. Thomas Aquinas (1226–1274), known as "the Angelic Doctor."

Canon 1366 of the Code of Church law declares: "Philosophy and theology shall be taught by the professors [in seminaries] absolutely according to the manner of the Angelic Doctor, without deviating from his doctrine and principles."

Thomism, the Philosophy of the Common Man

Thomism, or, to use a broader term, Scholasticism, is the philosophy elaborated by Aristotle and perfected in the service of Christian truth chiefly by the men who taught in the great universities from 1200 to the end of the eighteenth century. They are called the Schoolmen, or Scholastics.

The greatest work of St. Thomas is his *Summa Theologica,* a huge edifice of philosophical and theological knowledge, which fills at least three folio volumes. The whole work is divided into six parts; each part is divided into questions, or topics of inquiry; and each question is subdivided into articles. Part follows part, question grows out of question; one article is almost demanded by another. The *Summa* is truly a summation of all life.

The dry light of reason bathes the *Summa*, as it bathes all Scholastic philosophy and theology. There is no sarcasm, hardly any display of emotion, and only the driest humor. The title of each article is stated in the form of a question, for example: "Whether God's Existence Is Self-Evident?" This is followed by a number of objections, stated as fairly as if the Angelic Doctor were the Skeptic himself. Then comes the body of the article, and finally the replies to the objections.

The reader unaccustomed to certain philosophical terms will probably find St. Thomas hard at first; but, these learned, he will never fail to understand his meaning. Thomism is simply sublimated common sense. As a specimen of its reasoning I include here a condensation of article x, question 18, *Pars Tertia*, where Aquinas asks the question: "Whether Children of Jews or Other Unbelievers Should Be Baptized Against Their Parents' Will?"

"No—(a) The children of Jews or other unbelievers, who already have the use of reason, may be admonished and persuaded to receive Baptism, even against their parents' will; (b) but if they have not yet the use of reason the Church will not have such children baptized against their parents' wish.

"THE REASON OF THE FIRST is that children who have the use of reason already begin to control their own actions in things that are of divine and natural law; and therefore they can by their own will receive Baptism, against the wish of their parents, as they can also contract marriage.

"THE REASON OF THE SECOND is that, if they do not yet have the use of free will, they are, according to the natural law, under their parents' care as long as they cannot provide for themselves. And therefore it were against natural justice if such children were baptized against their parents' will. Nor should anyone violate the order of the natural law, whereby a child is under its father's care, in order to free it from the danger of eternal death. It would also be dangerous thus to baptize the children of unbelievers, because they would easily return to unbelief, on account of their natural affection for their parents."

Catholicity speaks in that short argument—Catholicity with its reasonableness and its respect for the dignity of man, which will not violate the law of nature even to save a man "from eternal death."

It is not pretended in the Catholic schools that St. Thomas Aquinas is infallible. Even one not too well versed in philosophy may now and then pick out an argument among the thousands in the *Summa* that does not ring quite true, or which at least can be answered differently. But in the main the Angelic Doctor says the last thing that can be said about a question, and the only task of the student is to understand him.

Thomism is not only the most catholic of philosophies, it is the most democratic of philosophies, in that it is the system of knowledge that most trusts the instincts of the common man. The common man believes that his senses generally give him accurate knowledge of the external world; so does the Thomistic philosopher. The common man believes that truth is attainable and that one truth cannot contradict another; in this he has the support of Thomism. The common man believes that every finite thing must have a cause, that nothing can just make itself. The philosopher who reasons in the tradition of Aristotle and Aquinas defends that conviction against its detractors.

Catholicity believes that God gave man his reason to use to the utmost of its capabilities. The first thing that follows from this is that he must reason accurately. All through Catholic philosophy and theology you find precision of definition and tightness of logic and clarity of language. Characteristic is the use of the syllogism, in which the major, the minor, and the conclusion are marshaled like a serried army. Here is an example:

Everything that shows signs of contrivance and design must be the work of a superior intelligence (the major or universal).

But the world shows signs of contrivance and design (the minor or particular).

Therefore the world is the work of a superior intelligence.

There is no possibility of sloppy thinking when one reasons in accurate syllogisms. The young man who studies in Catholic seminaries and colleges is taught by Thomistic philosophy to detect not only the arguments that lead to truth, but also the sophisms that lead reason astray.

Is Thomism Dogmatic?

Thomism is and must be dogmatic according to the accurate definition of philosophical dogmatism, which is the teaching of those who defend the objectivity of knowledge and the possibility and existence of certitude. Against skepticism, dogmatism holds that the first condition of certain knowledge is evidence, which necessarily holds the mind once it floods the reason with its light.

Some truths, such as the mysteries of faith, enjoy no immediate evidence in relation to us. Yet we can know their existence as certain and morally evident by the aid of revelation. Hence the mysteries of faith, which are evident to God, are only extrinsically evident to us, because they are accepted on account of evident testimony—for instance, the incomparable life of Christ or the miracles He performed. The Catholic Church teaches no truth without the evidence of authority, or the authority of evidence. A thing must be reasonable, or it is not Catholic.

Thomism teaches that human reason can, by its own native power, obtain a knowledge of many truths without the aid of faith; that human reason can demonstrate the foundations of faith, which are the prophecies and miracles of Christ, and the sanctity and wondrous diffusion of Catholicity throughout the world. Faith and reason exist together in the Christian, but the use of reason precedes the use of faith.

Faith, or the acceptance of the authority of God Revealing, is above reason and cannot be corrected by it, for faith teaches us some truths, such as the Trinity, the Incarnation, and the Real Presence of Our Lord in the Sacrament of the Altar, which exceed the limits of the human mind, but are not self-contradictory. Leo XIII, in his encyclical on the inspiration and inerrancy of Scripture (*Providentissimus*, 1893), declared that only "a false appearance of contradiction" can arise between faith and reason, either "from the fact that the dogmas of faith were not understood and expounded according to the mind of the Church, or false opinions are taken for the pronouncements of reason."

Leading Ideas of Catholic Philosophy

The first of these is the existence of absolute objective truth. Truth, in relation to us, is the conformity of the intellect with the thing that is known.

Every being is good. For every being is true, that is, is an object of the mind. A being that is not good for doing or receiving something could not be known. Moreover, every being, since it has some degree of perfection, is desirable as an end or means, either by the human will, or at least by God as willed and approved by Him. Hence the axiom: good is being, being is good. Manicheanism, the system that taught the evil of matter, has been fought by the Church, in one form or another, down through the centuries.

The theory of act and potentiality is the key arch on which the whole structure of Thomistic philosophy is built. In the strict sense, act is that by which a thing is determined and perfected. God is Pure Act because He is reality in supreme degree. Potentiality is a real capacity to do or suffer something; that is, it is something already existing in the thing or subject, ready to be brought into existence by act. Thus the oak exists potentially in the acorn.

Growing out of the doctrine of act and potentiality is the principle of sufficient reason, or causality. Nothing exists without a reason. Whatever is moved is moved by another— understand movement as any kind of change, such as the growth of a plant, a chemical transformation, or the act of a man in response to a thought. Nothing comes into act, or nothing is realized, unless it is moved by something that is already in act. The mover and the thing moved, or the cause of change and the subject of change, cannot be one and the same without self-contradiction.

This principle furnishes the most important ground for proving the existence of God. The world is finite, made up of parts, and subject to change. It is composed to potentiality and act. Therefore it is contingent—may be or may not be. Therefore it must have a cause, who is Pure Act, or God.

Parallel to the theory of potentiality and act is that of matter and form, of which all bodies are composed. In everything there is something to be determined, which remains the same (prime matter), and something that determines (substantial form). In man prime matter is the body, the form is the soul. In other words, the *soul* is what makes man, man; the body (matter) makes him this individual.

We now come to two words that are essential to an understanding of revelation, natural and supernatural. Natural is whatever corresponds to the needs, powers, and end of any individual nature or of all created or creatable beings. The human soul, for instance, which is sometimes inaccurately spoken of as "supernatural," is natural, because it is needed for the nature of man, who is by definition a creature composed of body and spiritual soul. Whatever the soul can do by itself is natural, and man's naturally proportioned end is natural.

Supernatural is that which exists above all nature, which is God. In relation to Him, we call supernatural the acts done by God outside the ordinary course of nature, e.g., the making of the blind to see, the resurrection of the dead.

This leads up to the definition of miracle, which is some fact done by God, whether immediately or through man or angel, but outside the ordinary course of the whole of created nature. Thus the sudden cure of cancer would be a miracle, because cures, natural in themselves, are outside the ordinary course of nature when done suddenly. Miracles are possible, since God can suspend the execution of His own laws, and they are discernible, since we can know what surpasses the powers of nature. It follows from this that revelation, which is attested by miracles and prophecies, can be made known to all intellects.

In concluding this chapter let me note again that, though Scholastic terminology may sound recondite, it represents mostly concepts familiar to any man. Take the division of causes into efficient, final, material, formal, and exemplar. A child before the age of reason can know that a chair is made to sit on (final cause), is made out of wood (material cause), is a chair because it is made in a chair's shape for a chair's purpose (formal cause), is made by a carpenter (efficient cause), from a design (exemplar cause).

Chapter 4

Man and God from Reason's Viewpoint

MAN is a composite of body and soul. The human soul is a spiritual substance, which is altogether simple. It is a substance because it is not the same as its powers of growth and nourishment, of sense and intellection, but is that in which these powers inhere and that which remains the same in consciousness and unconsciousness, always the subject of thoughts, memories, and sense impressions.

Spirit is a simple substance, which is so independent of matter that it can exist and live and act without it, and therefore can be separated from it. The soul is in itself independent of matter because it can do what matter cannot—reflect on itself, conceive universal ideas, such as a triangle, and think of objects that have nothing to do with matter, such as truth and beauty.

The soul is not a pure spirit, however, because its powers are extrinsically dependent on the organism for their exercise, though essentially they are independent. Without the body the soul cannot elicit any act of vegetative or sensitive life.

The soul is not the human person, for a person is the same as that which says *I*. Now that which says *I* is not the body alone, or the soul alone, but a composite of both. We say, for example, "*I* walked," not "my feet walked." Hence the soul separated from the body can indeed say *I*, but that *I* will be imperfect, indicating only a certain part of personality, though the most important part.

Body and soul constitute a single first principle, by which we act, but the soul, being spiritual and simple, is not informed by the body, but the body is informed by the soul. The soul gives being to the body.

The human soul is created in each human being at the moment of conception, immediately by God. Creation is necessary, since nothing spiritual can come from a material seed.

The essential characteristics of the human species are physical, intellectual, and moral. These are the same among all races. Therefore man is of the same species.

Being simple, the soul cannot be dissolved into parts, and, being spiritual, it has no absolute need for a material organ for the exercise of its proper life. Therefore it cannot perish. Moreover, a yearning that is universal in man must be natural, and whatever is natural must have the possibility of satisfaction. Since men yearn universally for immortality, there must be immortality, just as the instinct of birds to fly south argues the satisfaction of that instinct.

The Existence and Nature of God

We can conclude the existence of a Supreme Being from the maxim: everything that is moved (caused, changed) is moved by another. For the mover is in act; the movable thing, only in potentiality to act. Now it is impossible for the same thing to be in act and in potentiality at the same time under the same aspect, e.g., cold water cannot heat itself, a stick cannot move itself. It must have something that is already in act to change or move it. But there cannot be an infinite series of movers, for there cannot be intermediate things without extremes, and if there are extremes there can be no infinite series.

The existence of God is also proved from the existence of contingent beings, which demand a necessary, essential Being; from the wonderful order that exists in the universe, from the degrees of perfection that exist in the world, and from several other proofs that are not so often used.

We cannot define God, for He is not in any class or genus. He alone exists of Himself; all other things *have* existence from Him. But we can know something about Him by denying all imperfections of Him and affirming that He has all the perfections of creatures in an infinite degree.

The prime attribute of God, which is the root from which all others are derived, is aseity, or self-existence, without dependence on anything else. From this are derived God's infinity, absolute simplicity and immutability, His eternity, and presence in all things. The fact that God is absolutely beyond change does not mean that He is idle or inert. He is Pure Act, having infinite activity, moving but Himself unmoved. He is not a becoming, for He has no need to realize Himself. He has all the fullness of being. Since He has all perfections, He has both will and intelligence in an infinite degree. He is all-wise, all-seeing, all-good, all-just, all-holy. He is substantial Truth and Love. Men know things *because they exist*, love things *because they are good*. It is just the opposite with God, who knows and loves things *because He makes them*.

Since He possesses all good—indeed, is Goodness itself— God did not need to create, but if He does create He must create everything for His glory, since there can be no higher end than Himself. He creates out of love, out of the will to spread and communicate His goodness, but creation adds nothing to Him.

Since God is but one simple Act, unmixed with potentiality, His knowing is His being, His willing is His being, His loving is His being.

How, then, is man made in the image of God? In a sense, all creatures are made in the image of God, for every craftsman acts according to the ideas in his mind. In the case of God, these ideas are not different from His simple essence, which contains every perfection and the types of all things, somewhat as the Washington Monument is represented in many pictures, but remains one monument. Irrational creatures resemble God at least in being and goodness, or by way of trace, as the theologians say; men resemble God in their intellect, and this is called the resemblance of image.

In the parts of the universe, each creation is for the sake of its own perfection—the less noble for the nobler, namely man. The whole universe, with all its parts, is directed to God as its final end. But all the glory that creatures give to

God is for their benefit. God is the only true lover, for He alone gives all and receives nothing.

How far does God's providence extend? God cares for everything He creates, even the least. Nothing could exist, or continue in existence, or pass into act, unless He co-operated at every moment by His conserving action. But God cares in a special way for man, as being nearer to Him in his nature. There is a hierarchy of beings in the universe, whereby minerals serve plants, plants serve animals, animals serve man, and man, by giving God directly the honor that is due Him, serves his Creator. God did not create the best of possible worlds, for it is impossible for an infinite Being to produce the best—that would be to make another infinite God, a contradiction in terms. But the world He produced was the best *for His purpose.*

Physical evil is the absence of some perfection in a thing that should be there. God necessarily wills physical evil, since everything He creates must suffer some imperfection. But physical evil is only one side of physical good. A lion killing a deer intends food, which is good, though it involves the killing of an animal, which is a physical evil. God permits physical evil that the general good may benefit. Moral evil, which is sin, He never wills, but often permits, also for a higher good.

God's most proper name is He Who Is (Ex. iii, 14) or (what amounts to the same thing) Pure Act, as He was called by Aristotle in Book xi, Chapters 6 & 7 of his *Metaphysics.* He is the only Being who is His own existence, His own act, His own eternity. He alone is the rule of His own conduct.

Man's Last End

Thomistic Aristotelianism is a philosophy of ends. It is the nature of everything to act for the sake of an end, whether consciously or otherwise. Even inanimate beings act in some determinate way. Animal tissue heals itself when wounded, plants and animals brought into new varieties by fanciers tend to revert to type in the wild state. But man alone can direct himself to his end, since he has free will. This object of will is always some good. No man can act otherwise than for a good, real or apparent.

By "last end" we understand what is sought for its own sake. Other goods are sought as means to this end. What man seeks as his last end is his happiness; even if he would he cannot reject it. The question now arises: What constitutes man's happiness?

Happiness does not consist in the goods of the body—health, pleasure, money, luxuries. None of these excludes every evil. Besides, few men have them all in combination.

Neither does happiness consist in power, fame, honor, and glory. For one may have them all and still be miserable on account of ill health or ignorance.

Nor can knowledge make man happy, for it is deceptive and never complete. Virtue is not sufficient for happiness, since it is acquired and kept with difficulty and is compatible with physical evil. The fulfillment of duty cannot make us happy, for duty is a means, not an end. In brief, all the goods that draw the will of men suffer from this threefold defect: one may exist without the others; none is lasting; all, when possessed, sooner or later disappoint. Only an infinite Good can satisfy man. Man's final perfection can consist only in the operation that perfects his noblest faculties, namely the intellect and will. Therefore happiness must consist in the possession of God—possessed in the contemplation of the intellect and the love of the will.

We know from revelation that actually the last end of man consists in the face-to-face vision of the Divine Essence. But we are now considering the natural man, unaided by revelation. Man left to himself would never have possessed—perhaps never even have aspired to the possession of—such an ineffable vision. Nevertheless, his happiness would still be in God, only it would be via the natural powers of his intellect and will.

No man can escape his obligation to know and love God. There is a haunting line somewhere in Dante, which runs: "that Love, which excuses no man from loving." That stupendous obligation to love is the cause of all the restlessness as well as all the peace of man.

Although God alone is infinite good, and He alone can satisfy man, yet, because of the imperfect way in which He is necessarily apprehended in this life, man can react to Him as something inconvenient or as nonessential good, and repose the end of existence in creatures. But this does not hinder man from knowing, whenever he turns from his Highest Good, that nothing must come second to God. Since it is evident that there is no perfect happiness in the present life, even when God is loved, it follows that man must find the completion of his happiness in a state beyond this world. This happiness must be merited by acts done according to God's will, for God cannot reward deeds that are done contrary to the order He has established on this earth. This order, which rests in the very being of God, we call the eternal law.

Law, the Guide of Man

Law in general is defined by St. Thomas Aquinas as "an ordinance of reason for the common good, promulgated by him who has the care of the community." (*Summa,* Ia-IIae, q. 90, art. 1 & 2) Law is an ordinance of reason primarily, and only secondarily is it the result of will. An irrational or unjust law is no law.

The eternal law, which regulates all creation, Aquinas defines as "the rule of the divine wisdom insofar as it directs all acts and movements to their end." (*op. cit.,* Ia-IIae, q. 93, art. 1) God, once He creates, would not be wise if He knew no order; He would not be holy if He refused the order He knows; nor would He be a provident governor did He not impose on creatures the order they must follow.

Under the eternal law, which is the order God has impressed on creation, comes the natural law, which is the eternal law as it is made known to the consciences of men. The natural law, therefore, differs from the eternal law, as a law that is in both the lawgiver and his subjects differs from the law that is in the mind of the lawgiver only. It is important in arriving at an understanding of the natural law to dismiss any idea that it is connected with natural history. Only men can be subjects of the natural law. Because of its importance in moral theology, the natural law will be discussed in a later chapter.

Chapter 5

How Reason Determines Man's Duties

THE IMMEDIATE TEST of moral good or evil consists in the agreement or disagreeemnt of moral objects with human reason and, ultimately, with God's being. Therefore morality, like God Himself, is eternal, necessary, and immutable.

This foundation of morality on the reason and essence of God excludes all despotism in the divine order and puts it just in the human order. We say that a thing is good or evil because it is with or against the will of God; but God's will must always follow His intellect. Therefore there are some things that God Himself cannot do. For example, although He is the Master of life, He could not make murder or theft lawful. He could, of course, assert His primary rights as the Supreme Lord and owner of all things. Thus He could command Abraham to sacrifice Isaac, and this would not be murder. But God could not command anyone to do anything that is wrong by the very nature of the act; for instance, to tell the slightest lie really is a lie. No evil may be done, no matter how useful. The first principle of ethics is the axiom of the natural law: good is to be done and evil is to be avoided. This makes false all those ethical theories that are founded on self-interest or social good.

A good act may be not only that which is known directly from the natural law, but also that which is in accordance with the positive law of man, for all laws hold authority from the eternal law.

What Are the Duties of Man?

The principal duties of man are toward God, himself, and his neighbor. Since man was meant for God he is bound by his very nature to fulfill the duties of religion, which is the sum of all the obligations that bind the rational creature to his Creator. Religion must be professed in acts, both internal and external, which constitute the exercise of worship. Since God is Lord of the whole man, body and soul, we must express our adoration not only with our minds but also with our bodies. We are bound to pay worship to God in thanksgiving to Him as the Giver of all gifts. Supposing we have gravely offended God by sin, we are bound to express repentance and placate Him in some manner, namely by sacrifice.

Since God made man, He, as the Supreme Author, Ruler, and End of creation, made all the things that necessarily follow from the nature of man. Now the association of men in civil society is a necessary consequence of man's social nature. Hence God is also the Author, Ruler, and End of the state, which is bound to pay Him social worship.

Since man's intellect is his highest faculty, his first duties are to it. This means that he is bound to pursue the true and reject the false. Hence absolute freedom of thought is false and pernicious. No one can do right unless he thinks right. That is why, although the state may tolerate error for the sake of a higher good, nature demands that we refrain from the grave danger of going mentally astray. One may err in good faith, and in that case he must follow his conscience, but he has a duty to correct his conscience if he seriously suspects he is in error. There can be no natural liberty to read or hear anything one pleases.

Untenable is the idea of freedom of conscience that holds that man has the right to do anything that does not injure his neighbor. The individual conscience cannot be substituted for the eternal law. If it were morally right to think, write, and teach anything one pleases, man would not depend on God but would be a law unto himself.

There can be no right to teach atheism, or any social doctrine that subverts the common good, such as Communism. Atheistic teachers are morally illiterate and therefore incompetent to teach. Even the citizens of Utopia were not allowed unlimited freedom of expression. Thomas More, after relating that King Utopus "gave to everye man free libertie and choise to believe what he would," added the qualifying phrase: "savinge that he earnestlye and straitelye charged them, that no man should conceave so vile and base an opinion of the dignitie of mans nature, as to think that the soules do die and perish with the bodye; or that the world runneth at all aventures governed by no divine providence." (Raphe Robynson translation, edited by J. Rawson Lumby, Cambridge, 1940, p. 147)

The right of dominion over things is legitimate and natural. For by the order of Providence the lesser things were intended to relieve the needs of individual men, and therefore all things were created to be appropriated.

The reason for this is that the life and liberty of the individual cannot be maintained without individual ownership. Therefore man may rightly appropriate whatever is in nature that belongs to nobody. Another reason for ownership, established in the natural law, is the fact that wealth is in a very real sense the extension of man's own personality. "For when man spends the industry of his mind and the strength of his body in procuring the fruits of nature, by that act he makes his own that portion of nature's field that he cultivates—that portion on which he leaves, as it were, the impress of his own personality. . . . A family, no less than a state, is a true society, governed by a power within itself, that is, by the father. Wherefore . . . the family has at least equal rights with the state in the choice and pursuit of those things that are needful to its preservation and its just liberty." (Leo XIII, *Rerum Novarum,* p. 6)

The right of property must, however, be tempered by the grave obligation to use it for the common good. For were there an unlimited right to the goods of nature, a few owners would grow inordinately rich and the masses would be impoverished, as has happened in so many countries. Ownership is not, however, merely a social function, valid only on condition that property be used for the benefit of the poor. On the contrary, every man's ownership over his own property is something personal and absolute. The possessive instinct is to be regulated neither by humanitarianism nor by social prudence to forestall revolution, but by the order of charity, whereby we love our neighbor for the sake of God.

A corollary of this is that Socialism is untenable, and contrary to natural morality. "Our first and most fundamental principle," writes Leo XIII in *Rerum Novarum,* "must be the inviolability of private property." (*Ibid.,* p. 7)

Between proletarianization and extreme wealth, there stands a middle course, namely a system of free associations, in which nonpolitical corporations of employers and employees in the same factory or industry regulate the production and distribution of goods according to the higher norms of justice. This will reconcile the right of private property with the necessity of collective action.

The Family and Education

The family is the stable union of a man and woman with their children under the government of the man. That is natural to which nature inclines and God commands. Now we know how God wants the species propagated from the nature of the needs of the offspring who, unlike the lower animals, need the care of both mother and father for a long period of years, and hence require to live in a stable society. Thus the family is derived from the natural law and is essentially independent of the state, both because civil society is a kind of extension of families, and therefore comes after the family in time and the order of nature, and because the family is directed to things that are absolutely necessary; namely, generation and education, whereas civil society is directed only to the things that come in second place, i.e., the common prosperity of families.

Since the family is a society, and every society must have rulers and ruled, it is natural that the position of ruler should fall on the man, who is the breadwinner and is best suited by strength of will and bent of intellect to command. The man, therefore, is head of the family, and the woman is his companion, but not his slave.

This subordination of the wife to the husband denotes no natural inferiority, for all those who possess human nature are essentially equal. It merely means that the capacities required for ruling a family do not naturally, for many reasons, center in a woman, whose sex fits her to be queen and not king. Experience has shown, especially in Soviet Russia and the Iron Curtain countries, that the false economic and political equality of woman debases her.

To Whom Does Education Belong?

Since the parents beget children and supply them with bodily nurture, to them also belongs the right and duty of their spiritual development. Children are, as it were, an extension of the parents' personality. Only they can give them a natural love. Only they can, as a rule, establish between their children and themselves the psychological bond that is so necessary in imparting moral instruction, which children need most of all. Intellectual culture is not the primary part of their development.

Before the French Revolution no one asked the question: Education, to whom does it belong? Everyone, even among the pagan Greeks, took it for granted that it belonged naturally to the parents, who used schools only as extensions of the training they themselves gave within the family circle. Schoolmasters and professors were regarded as the agents of the parents, commissioned by them to do work that they themselves could not perform. Always it was the parents who had the final responsibility of education. Parents chose freely their schools, and teachers were paid by the families. The state did not interfere. (Ciarlantini, *The Liberty of the School and Family Education,* pp. 53–62)

Not even the most radical Communist state would think of dictating how its subjects should eat. Yet the movements of the will and intellect are at least as much a part of man as his digestive system. The state has no more right to claim a monopoly of schools than it has to claim a monopoly of breakfast-food factories. Education is a natural complement to generation. Parents did not bring their children into the world by command of the state; neither, therefore, should the state have the right to dictate how they should be brought up. Is doctrine or moral teaching important in the child's life? Who is to say they are not? The state? If it does, it arrogates to itself a function that it does not have and by its nature cannot have.

The state has the right to expect, and an interest in cultivating, the willing co-operation of all citizens in the commonwealth. It cannot achieve this end unless moral character is built into its citizens, and this can be done only by moral education imparted directly by the family, or indirectly through schools of its choice. The state rightly subsidizes housing projects to provide lodging at reasonable rents for poor families. If it can help the material needs of the family, it can help its spiritual needs, by subsidizing either the school of the parents' choice or the child, enabling him to attend the school to which his parents direct him.

"The function therefore of the civil authority residing in the State is twofold, to protect and to foster, but by no means to absorb, the family and the individual, or to substitute itself for them. . . .

"It belongs also to the State to protect the rights of the child itself when the parents are found wanting, either physically or morally in this respect. . . . Their right to educate is not an absolute and despotic one, but dependent on the natural and divine law." (Pius XI, *On the Christian Education of Youth*, from *Five Great Encyclicals*, pp. 48–49)

Civil Authority and God

Civil society, or the state, is the permanent union of many families under the same government for the pursuit of the common temporal good. Since man cannot attain his due perfection outside the state, the state must be regarded as a natural society, inferior to the family as being its effect, but able to command families for the common good. Cicero thus expresses this formation of the state by a natural concretion of families: "The first society consisted in wedlock itself, and then in its children; afterwards there was one household, in which all things were in common; this was the beginning of a city and the seedplot of the commonwealth." (*De Officiis*, Book I, Chapter vii)

Hence, being an effect of man's nature, the state is indirectly established by God and is given to men as a property that follows from their nature. Thus, also, since it does not depend on man what nature he shall have, so the political power is outside the consent of man and derives from natural divine law. In this way it differs from all subordinate associations, such as a commercial company or a university, since these derive from the agreement of men.

"As no society," wrote Leo XIII, "can hold together unless someone be over all, directing all to strive earnestly for the common good, every civilized community must have a ruling authority, and this authority, no less than society itself, has its source in nature, and consequently has God for its Author." (*Christian Constitution of States*, p. 3)

How did political authority arise? The majority of modern Scholastics, notably St. Robert Bellarmine and Francisco Suarez, affirm that it was conferred indirectly, through the people. St. Thomas also declared that it "belongs to the community to make laws." (*Summa,* Ia-IIae, q. 90, art. 3, ad 3; q. 97, art. 3, ad 3)

Aquinas declared: "The ruler has power and eminence from the subjects, and, in the event of his despising them, he sometimes loses both his power and position" (*De Eruditione Principum,* Book i, cap. 6).

St. Robert Bellarmine declared, 150 years before our republic was founded, that "it depends on the consent of the multitude to constitute over itself a king, consul, or other magistrate. This power is, indeed, from God, but vested in a particular ruler by the counsel and election of men." (*De Laicis,* c. 6, notes 4 and 5) "The people themselves immediately and directly hold the political power." (*De Clericis,* cap. 7)

What is the best form of government? This question cannot be decided in the concrete by recourse to the natural law. In general, that form of government is best which best fits the character of the people. A republic, for instance, has not worked in Spain, but a strong monarchy has been successful. A rather pure form of democracy seems suitable for Switzerland. It is doubtful whether the federal system is so well adapted to Mexico as to the United States, etc.

In the abstract, however, the natural philosophy and tradition of Catholicity have certainly a preference for monarchy (in the United States the federal government is essentially a monarchy). A society with a single head is stronger, more peaceful, and more in conformity with nature, since it imitates the monarchical organization of the family. St. Thomas writes: "What is one in itself can be the cause of unity more aptly than many units will be." (*Summa,* I, q. 103, art. 3) History has proved that monarchies (including the United States) have had a more stable and happier existence than have pure democracies or aristocracies.

What are the duties and limitations of the state? Fundamental in Catholic philosophy is the principle of pluralism, which says that the state must not engross the whole of man's activities but should to the utmost favor subordinate societies, such as occupational groups. The Church has always defended labor unions, for instance, as deriving their rights from the natural law, which gives man, independently of any right conferred by the state, the moral power to organize to achieve his legitimate aims.

But the state in Catholic thought is not a mere policeman; it has for its end everything that is necessary to attain the common good, namely the intellectual and moral, as well as the physical, welfare of the people. From this it follows that the state has the right to bind the consciences of its subjects to obey its laws. Beyond this mandate the state may not go, and if it presumes to touch matters that involve the very nature of man, such as his right to the integrity of the body or the family's right to the education of its children, it trespasses its limits and acts unjustly.

The state can do many things for the social welfare of its citizens, such as regulating the rate of interest, fixing prices where necessary, prescribing decent conditions of labor, and fixing a minimum wage scale. It should encourage arts and industry, but it is not ordinarily its duty to build factories, engage in commerce, cultivate fields, and the like, which are better left to private enterprise. Still less has it a mandate to undertake the education of all the people. The end of the state is not to supplant the initiative of its citizens, but to stimulate and advance it.

The Church makes its own the Oregon decision of the United States Supreme Court, handed down June 22, 1925: "The fundamental theory of liberty, upon which all governments in this Union repose, excludes any general power of the State to standardize its children by forcing them to accept instruction from public teachers only. The child is not a mere creature of the State; those who nurture him and direct his destiny have the right, coupled with high duty, to recognize and prepare him for additional duties." These words were quoted by Pius XI in his encyclical *Christian Education of Youth*.

Chapter 6

The Church Teaching

ACCORDING to the will of Christ, the Church has the exclusive right to teach His revealed word. This power to teach includes infallibility, which means that the Church cannot teach false doctrine or lead the faithful into ways not pleasing to God.

Infallibility follows from the nature of the Church as a

society that cannot fail. In 1870 the Vatican Council declared what this meant: "We define that the Roman Pontiff, when he speaks *ex cathedra*—i.e., when in discharging his office of shepherd and teacher of all Christians he determines, in accordance with his supreme Apostolic authority, that a doctrine of faith or morals must be held by the entire Church—we define that in so speaking he enjoys through the divine assistance . . . that infallibility with which the Divine Redeemer wished His Church to be endowed in defining a doctrine of faith or morals; and therefore that the definitions of the same Roman Pontiff are by their very nature, and not by reason of the Church's consent, irreformable." (Denz., 1839)

For the exercise of this infallible authority, the Roman Pontiff must speak, not as a private teacher or as Bishop of the city of Rome or as a civil ruler, but as the shepherd and teacher of the whole Church, in the exercise of his supreme authority; he must teach a truth of faith or morals; and he must definitely determine what things must be held with a truly internal faith. Finally, he must intend that his definition bind the entire Church.

Hence the Pope cannot be infallible in determining the burial place of Peter (though Pius XII seemed to speak as though it had been found), or in discoursing about the age of the universe before the Pontifical Academy of Science.

No particular form need be observed in an infallible Papal document. An allocution, such as any one of the eighty-odd addresses the Pope makes every year, can, in itself, be infallible; so also can an encyclical, or a brief to a single Bishop. It is because of the absence of any necessary form for an infallible pronouncement that you will hardly find two authors in agreement as to their number. *Dictionaire de la théologie catholique,* for example, mentions only eleven Papal documents that are indisputably *ex cathedra.* (Tome VII, col. 1703 et seq.) Most encyclicals, however, contain doctrine that was previously pronounced with infallibility by Popes and councils. Much controversy, moreover, about the *ex cathedra* character of many Papal pronouncements is purely academic. Theologians still dispute, for example, whether the condemnations of certain abuses of marriage in the encyclical *Casti Connubii* constitute *ex cathedra* definitions. The dispute is academic, since it is always true that, even if it be not a dogma of faith, doctrine promulgated by the Pope is infallibly true by the fact of his declaring solemnly and authoritatively a moral doctrine that in every age was constantly proposed by the ordinary teaching office of the

Universal Church as surely to be held and observed in the practice of Christian life. (Cartechini, *Dall' Opinione al Domma,* pp. 37–38)

Although some Papal statements are admittedly not infallible, if they are directed to the Universal Church on a matter of faith or morals they are binding in conscience. Pius XII, in his encyclical *Humani Generis,* issued in 1950, explains the matter thus:

"Nor is it to be supposed that a position advanced in an encyclical does not, by that very fact, claim assent. In writing them, it is true, the Popes do not exercise their teaching authority to the full. But such statements come under the day-to-day teaching of the Church [this is called the ordinary Magisterium], which is covered by the promise: 'He who listens to you, listens to Me' [Luke x, 16]. For the most part the positions advanced, the duties inculcated, by these encyclical letters are already bound up, under some other title, with the general body of Catholic teaching. And when the Roman Pontiffs go out of their way to pronounce on some subject, which has hitherto been controverted, it must be clear to anybody that, in the mind and intention of the Pontiffs concerned, this subject can no longer be regarded as a matter of free debate among theologians." (Knox translation)

The Sovereign Pontiff is the only officer of the Church who by himself possesses the prerogative of infallibility. But the Bishops dispersed throughout the world, and forming one moral body with the Roman Pontiff, possess infallibility in their day-to-day teaching. That is, the Bishops, as long as they are in communion with the Church of Rome, cannot teach any doctrine that would mislead the faithful. They may indeed fail as individual teachers, but all of them together cannot teach anything contrary to faith.

Most infallible decisions of the Church have not been made by the Sovereign Pontiffs alone, but in union with world-wide, or ecumenical, councils, to which are summoned Cardinals, Bishops, and Archbishops, and Abbots. As regards the conduct of the business of the council, the Roman Pontiff must preside over the sessions, either personally or through his delegates. It is not required that all the Bishops of the Catholic world meet together; it is enough if, morally speaking, the whole Church is represented. Unanimous consent is not required. If disagreement persists among them that part of the Bishops will be infallible who, though they be in a minority, adhere to the Sovereign Pontiff, since he is unable to err in a matter of faith or morals.

General councils are not absolutely necessary, but are of

great utility, because they exhibit greater human authority than the Pope alone. They afford the Roman Pontiff, moreover, a means of determining revealed doctrine and of seeking out the views of the Bishops regarding the best means of correcting abuses or promoting virtue. It cannot be emphasized too often that the prerogative of Papal infallibility does not mean the power to govern despotically or freedom from the necessity of study. The dogma of the Immaculate Conception, proclaimed in 1854, was prepared for by theological discussion reaching back through eight centuries.

Infallibility must not be confused with inspiration, such as was possessd by the writers of Sacred Scripture. It is not universal knowledge. It takes often many centuries before a doctrine has jelled sufficiently for definition. No men on earth have worked harder or longer than have theologians in clearing up some point of dogma.

This answers the question some naive people ask from time to time. If the Roman Church is infallible, say they, why does it not publish an infallible commentary of all the verses of Scripture? Why does it jealously refuse the light that it could give to souls by defining exactly the meaning of obscure passages?

The answer is that infallibility takes away error, not ignorance. Catholics do not recognize even in the head of the Church the gift of prophecy or the power to make new revelations. The Church respects the intellect, and she teaches that God is not lavish with miracles. To attempt to define any point of doctrine before it has been carefully thought out would be a temptation of God.

Infallibility, finally, is not the power to reveal new truth. It simply means that the Pope and Bishops cannot, when they wish to teach the entire Church, make a mistake in determining what was held by the Apostles. The Church teaches that divine revelation came to an end with the death of the last of the Apostles, St. John. Her teaching authority is one of interpretation and definition only. The subject matter of Christian doctrine is as fixed as the stars. The Pope can no more create a new dogma than an astronomer can create a heavenly body. An astronomer may demonstrate that what was thought to be one star is really two. The Pope can define that the doctrine of the bodily presence of the Mother of God in heaven is contained in the fact that Mary was a mother worthy of God, and, like her Son, with whom she co-operated, could not fittingly know the corruption of the grave. But all this was held in the Church, at least implicitly, from the beginning.

Need I say that infallibility is not the power to declare good evil, or evil good, and that it confers no power to pronounce on civil or scientific matters, which are outside the jurisdiction of the Church?

The Church—more than any other institution in history—is alive, and a living thing is always in act. The Church's dogmas never change, but they may and do grow in the understanding of Catholics. What is a theological opinion today may be declared a dogma at some future date, although what has once been declared a dogma can never become again an opinion.

The field of faith, which includes all Catholic dogmas, is relatively restricted. The field of theology, which embraces speculation in connection with dogmas, is very wide. Some of the conclusions of theology are certain, and guaranteed by the infallible teaching office of the Church; many others are free and more or less probable opinions, which may be discarded as theological science develops.

According to the explicitness with which they are contained in revelation, theological truths are graded thus: (1) Those that are held on divine faith alone, i.e., those few dogmas that lie on the surface of Scripture and that even non-Catholics may believe with divine faith, for example, the Divinity of Christ. (2) Those that are held with Catholic faith, which are contained in either Scripture or Divine Tradition and proposed by the Church as objects of faith. The term dogma is properly applied to all revealed matter proposed by the Church as of divine faith, all those truths the contradictories of which have been condemned as heretical, and all those truths so plainly contained in Scripture that they cannot possibly be doubted.

Proximate to faith are those propositions that are regarded as divinely revealed by the majority of theologians, but not defined by the Church. Theologically certain is a truth that is admitted by all the Catholic schools as intimately connected with revelation. Thus it is deduced from the fact that the Father, Son, and Holy Spirit are one God that they are "consubstantial," i.e., have the same nature. "Catholic doctrine" is the name given to a proposition that is taught in the whole Catholic Church by the official teaching authority and in all the Catholic schools. For example, it is Catholic doctrine that the propositions contained in Papal encyclicals demand assent. In fact, "Catholic doctrine" covers the very wide field of the matters taught by the Popes and Bishops in the day-to-day exercise of their teaching office. Whether or not "Catholic doctrine" is infallible must be determined by the context in which it appears, but it always demands implicit and wholehearted assent.

Although the Church cannot err in establishing the truth of moral laws and principles, she can make a mistake in applying her disciplines. An egregious example was the temporary dissolution of the Society of Jesus under Clement XIV. The Church never claims more than probability in approving private revelations.

It can happen that an opinion, classified as more probable than another—even one that claims the common assent of theologians—can turn out to be false. But this is so only in those propositions that the Church does not believe with divine or Catholic faith. When the Universal Church holds some truth of faith as certain she is infallible. An example is the bodily presence of Mary in heaven, regarded as certain for centuries before it was defined.

All doctrines are designated as heretical if they are directly contradictory to a truth revealed by God and proposed to Catholics as such by the Church. A denial of the dogma of the Assumption before 1950 would have been a mortal sin, but it would not have been heretical in the strict sense, because until that year it had not been proclaimed as a truth of divine and Catholic faith.

Going down through degrees of probability, we have, after certain theological conclusions, propositions that are called "common and certain." For example, it is a dogma that the sacraments confer grace. No one may deny that without heresy. But it is only "common and certain" today that the sacraments bestow grace as causes and not merely as conditions. A "common and certain" statement of a theological fact can be called practically certain. (Cartechini, *Dall' Opinione al Domma*, p. 132)

The Church has her opinions, and does not admit everything as if it were of Catholic faith. Take the widespread belief in the early Church in the imminent second coming of Christ. That was a probable opinion then; today it lacks all probability and is false. A proposition that is today evidently false has no probability, even if it was held by great ancient authors. An example would be belief in the geographical universality of the Deluge, which was widely held in the first centuries.

The Church reveres the past but does not worship it. She willingly admits that a theologian of much lesser genius than Augustine or Thomas Aquinas could today, after having the benefits of so many Church councils, see better and say something truer than those giant intellects said in their day.

Another vast field of opinions is classified as "safe," or the opposite. Thus it is not safe to deny the existence of physical fire in hell, although in early centuries it was denied by the great Origen. Anything contained in an encyclical is at least *safe*.

Thus Catholic doctrine is continually developing in our understanding of it, as I shall explain more fully later. But the truths themselves do not depend on our fullness of understanding. Hence Catholics in the twentieth century believe the same truths as were believed in the first century, though perhaps more explicitly.

Chapter 7

From Tradition to Scripture

THERE ARE two sources from which the Catholic learns the spoken word of God. The first is divine or divine-Apostolic Tradition, which is the revealed word of God transmitted orally from Christ to the Apostles, or received by the Apostles through the inspiration of the Holy Spirit, according to the promise of Christ: "The Paraclete, the Holy Spirit . . . will teach you all things, and bring all things to your mind, whatsoever I shall have said to you." (John xiv, 26)

Tradition is said to be *unwritten* in the sense that it was not written under divine inspiration. That infants are validly baptized, for example, is Tradition, because it is not contained in any *written* inspired work, although it is recorded in the works of nearly all ancient ecclesiastical writers. (Parente, *Dictionary of Dogmatic Theology*, art. "Tradition")

What is called *active Tradition* is nothing less than the Magisterium of the Church transmitting Apostolic doctrine and interpreting Scripture from age to age.

Nothing like the Magisterium exists in the world, or has existed. No religion other than the Catholic comes forward with the statement: "I am a society of divine foundation, possessed of the power to reply to question after question upon the only things that really matter, to which questions man has never yet of himself attained an answer. . . . I alone am the voice of God perpetually speaking, settling controversies, defining and redefining in ever-expanding areas of thought whatever truths may be challenged." (Belloc, *Catholic Church and History*, pp. 103–104)

The second source of revelation is Holy Writ, which the Magisterium infallibly interprets, as it does Tradition. The Catholic, therefore, knows no hostility between Tradition and Scripture, such as Protestants often conceive there to be. Both are subjected to the same living word of God, the teaching office of the Church.

Tradition, both active and passive, came before Scripture in point of time, for the Church, instructed and guided by the living word of the Apostles, already existed before Christ's revelations were consigned to inspired books. At least forty years were to pass between the writing of the first and the writing of the last of the books of the New Testament. Thousands of people became Christians through the work of the Apostles and their aids, and Christianity had become a world religion before ever they saw or read, or possibly could see or read, a single sentence of inspired Writ from the New Testament. (Graham, *Where We Got the Bible,* pp. 18–19)

All the books of the Bible, moreover, were not determined and collected until 397, when the Council of Carthage settled the canon, or collection of New Testament Scriptures, as they are known today and sent them on to Rome for confirmation. The Epistles of James and Jude, the Second Epistle of Peter, the Second and Third of John, the Epistle to the Hebrews, and the Apocalypse of John were disputed for generations by even the greatest Scriptural scholars. On the other hand, there was a class of books thought by some to be inspired, which are not now recognized as part of the Bible by either Protestants or Catholics.

Tradition also is superior to Scripture in completeness. For active Tradition preserves not only the entire written word of God, insofar as the Sacred Books have been transmitted to posterity by the active Tradition of the Church, but also certain truths that are mentioned only cursorily in Scripture, so that without the testimony of the oral teaching of the Apostles they would scarcely be recognized as revealed truths. Examples are the observance of Sunday as the Lord's Day and the authorship and inspired character of many books of the Bible.

Finally, Tradition enjoys greater independence than Scripture. For the credibility of Tradition and the truth of the doctrines therein contained can be determined by infallible judgment independently of Scripture, once you grant that the successors of Peter and the Apostles enjoy the protection of the Holy Spirit. Holy Writ in all its parts cannot be known as a source of revelation without the witness of Tradition, and therefore it depends on it. It is a source of never-failing wonder to Catholics that so many Protestants cannot understand this.

It is freely acknowledged by Catholics, however, that there are some respects in which Scripture greatly excels oral Tradition. One such reason has already been mentioned as inspiration, by virtue of which Holy Writ has God for its Author. The texts of Tradition have as their authors only such men as were guided by the divine assistance but were not inspired. Scripture is also sometimes clearer than Tradition, and easier to understand, inasmuch as the words of Apostolic Tradition as originally uttered are no longer extant, and the doctrine it contains is transmitted by various means that individually are not gifted with infallibility. But what is beyond the reach of private theologians is accessible to the divinely guided Magisterium, which can safely interpret both Tradition and Scripture. We by no means say, of course, that the divine assistance excludes common foresight and the use of natural and ordinary means for the study of revelation. In fact, it supposes it.

How does the Magisterium know what was preached and believed in every previous age? The preaching of the Church in every age has left permanent traces, destined to endure for many centuries. It is recorded in records and monuments of various sorts, and in these can be made known to posterity.

There are, first of all, the ancient creeds: The Apostles' Creed, whose doctrine is certainly Apostolic; and the Creed of Nicea-Constantinople, issued first by the Council of Nicea (325) and afterward completed by the Council of Constantinople (381). There are the definitions of Councils and Roman Pontiffs. Then we have the ancient liturgies, which record the worship, and therefore the faith, of the early centuries. We have the acts of the martyrs, some of which date to the second century, from which we discover the faith that stayed the first Christians as they went to their death.

Finally, in an ever-widening stream, we have the writings of the Fathers of the early Church, beginning with the *Didache,* or Teaching of the Twelve, written in the last decade of the first century; the letters of Ignatius, martyred in the year 107; the Apology of Justin, who died in 163; the Epitaph of Abercius, which records the faith in the Real Presence and the pre-eminence of the See of Rome; the writings of Irenaeus (140–202) against the Gnostics; and so on.

But the Magisterium of the Church, when it delivers any definition, can base itself on documents establishing only the present explicit consent of Catholics, even if it finds no explicit document written by the Fathers of the Church. Thus the dogma of seven sacraments became explicit only after the early ages. (Cartechini, *Dall' Opinione al Domma,* p. 249)

Who Were the Fathers of the Church?

The name *Father* is given to the men, conspicuous for learning and sanctity, who illuminated the Church by their writings from the first to about the eighth centuries. The greatest of the Fathers were St. Jerome (345–420) and St. Augustine (354–430), but there were men of somewhat lesser attainments who came before and after them. Such were Cyprian (third century), Chrysostom (fourth century), Vincent of Lerins (fifth century), Isidore of Seville (sixth century), and the Damascene (eighth century).

When the Fathers affirm with practical unanimity that a certain doctrine was divinely revealed they are considered as infallible and their conclusions are binding on all. The reason for this is that all the authoritative teachers of one Christian age could not err in faith without leading the whole Church astray, and the Church is indefectible.

Subsidiary to the argument from the consent of the Fathers is the argument from prescription, which goes as follows: If a certain doctrine (e.g., the primacy of the Roman Bishops) can be shown to have been taught without contradiction in the Church in a certain century (e.g., the fifth) there is no sufficient reason for this fact save that the doctrine was held from the time of the Apostles. For in every age learned, holy, and vigilant writers flourished who brought to light every new (and therefore heretical) doctrine and mercilessly persecuted it.

The heresiarch always appears as an innovator to the generation whom he disturbs. There is not one case, as Hilaire Belloc observes, in the long history of the Church where we can trace a steady protest against any one of her fundamental doctrines. Nor is there any one case of a definition of orthodox doctrine appearing suddenly and with all the effect of innovation. (*Catholic Church and History,* pp. 77–78)

Next to that of the Fathers comes the authority of the theologians. A theologian, in proper Catholic usage, is one who, by commission of the Church or with her approval, scientifically determines what is revealed truth and what conclusions can be drawn from it. He is usually, but not necessarily, a Bishop or priest. The unanimous consent of the theologians approved by the Church in any one age renders their judgments theologically certain.

A special approval is given by the Pontiffs to the teachings of St. Thomas Aquinas, whom we met in our review of

Catholic philosophy. The Church does not guarantee every proposition of the great Schoolman. In disputed matters in Catholic theology, as for instance whether the saved are in a majority or a minority, no one is bound to follow his opinion. The presumption, however, is in favor of his arguments if he proposes them as certain and not merely as free opinion, or unless present knowledge has rendered his theses untenable (which is rarely the case).

Do the Catholic People Have Any Influence on the Determination of Doctrine?

The Catholic Church, in at least one respect, is a greater democracy than any that has ever existed: it accords the dead a vote. The judgment of the ancient Fathers and the early Christian people is never to be lightly set aside. The Catholic theologian, in assessing the claims of articles of doctrine, must always have before him what has been said by St. Thomas, St. Bonaventure, Suarez, and other luminaries. He may not rule out any authentic voice because it is centuries old. But even the faithful—and the word *faithful* can include not only laymen, who belong to the Church Learning, but even Bishops and Pontiffs, insofar as they privately believe what they teach or profess—are in a real sense infallible in matters of faith and morals.

When the Church Universal—laity, priests, and prelates—believes with a clear and certain faith something in faith or morals that is held either explicitly or implicitly, in practice and custom, then the consent of the whole Christian people is a firm criterion of divine truth. (Herve, *Manuale Theologiae Dogmaticae*, I, N. 595)

Thus one of the best assurances we have for the early belief in original sin comes with a knowledge of the constant (though at first infrequent) practice of infant Baptism. Pius IX, before defining the dogma of Mary's Immaculate Conception December 8, 1854, asked the Bishops to indicate "what was the piety and devotion of their faithful regarding the Immaculate Conception of the Mother of God"; and innumerable were the signatures taken up throughout the Catholic world begging that the Assumption be declared a dogma to be believed with divine and Catholic faith.

The universal belief in the Assumption for eight centuries in both the Eastern and the Western branches of the Church afforded the strongest reason for its being proclaimed as implicitly revealed; else the Church would have fallen into error on a matter of faith, contrary to the promises of Christ.

Indeed, although the Sovereign Pontiff is infallible by himself, and Councils, Bishops, and theologians are infallible when they teach unanimously under him, the Church Teaching is by no means a despotic thing. For the Pontiff and the other teachers of the Church themselves teach and define the truth as it is learned from all. "Indeed, God may sometimes use the faithful to promote some form of worship, e.g., the cultus of the Sacred Heart of Jesus." (Tanquerey, *Brevior*, N. 287) It is not true, of course, that the Church Teaching merely sanctions the opinions of the Church Learning, but the determination of dogma, even with, or because of, the aid of the Holy Spirit, is a delicate thing, and God sometimes makes the sense of the faithful an occasion for definitions or the rejection of errors.

What Does the Church Teach About the Truth of Scripture?

The Catholic Church holds, as of divine faith, that all the books of the Old and the New Testaments were written under the inspiration of the Holy Spirit, and thus have God for their Author. (Denz., 706, 783, 1787, 2, 009)

This inspiration need not demand that the sacred author have been aware of God's inspiring hand, still less that he have written without labor, in an ecstasy or trance. It is not even necessary that the inspired book have been written by the author whose name it bears. Inspiration is a supernatural divine influence on the imagination and intellect and will of the man who was moved and excited to write certain things in God's name and in the manner in which God wills.

God excites and moves the writer to write and assists him as he writes. He provides the human writer with supernatural light, by means of which he correctly conceives in his mind what God wishes to be written. God continues to give him His assistance, so that he will not fall into any error. (Tanquerey, N. 293)

The inerrancy of Holy Writ follows from its divine inspiration, since God cannot deceive or be deceived. Scripture is absolutely inerrant in the sense in which it is meant to be taken. This does not mean, however, that the sense is always easy to determine.

Always to be borne in mind is the literary type according to which the Hebrew author wrote, who had different conceptions of historiography from that of the classical and modern historians. Thus Catholics are free to believe that the books of Job and Jonas are either literal history or divinely inspired parables, declaring the mercy and goodness of God and His will to save all men. (*Conway's Question Box*, pp. 75–76)

In a letter sent to the Archbishop of Paris from the Pontifical Commission on Biblical Studies, January 16, 1948, it was clearly laid down that the first eleven chapters of Genesis come under the heading of history; in what exact sense, it is for the further labors of the exegete to determine. "These chapters have a *naif,* symbolical way of talking, well suited to the understanding of a primitive people. But they do disclose to us certain important truths, upon which the attainment of our eternal salvation depends, and they do also give a popularly-written description of how the human race, and the chosen people in particular, came to be. It may be true that these old writers of sacred history drew some of their material from the stories current among the people of their day. So much may be granted; but it must be remembered on the other side that they did so under the impulse of divine inspiration, which preserved them from all error in selecting and assessing the material they used. These excerpts from current stories, which are found in the sacred books, must not be put on a level with mere myths, or with legend in general." (Pius XII, in his encyclical, *Humani Generis,* Knox translation)

Recurrent in the writings of ecclesiastical authors, however, is the emphasis that it was not the sacred writer's intention to record scientific truth; he was content with describing things according to their external appearances, so as to be understood by all. "The Spirit of God," writes St. Augustine, "who spoke through the sacred writers, did not intend to teach men what was in no wise profitable for their salvation." (*De Genesi ad Litteram*, III, 9, 20)

Because Scripture is a divine book, only a divinely constituted teaching authority can finally decide its meaning. The Vatican Council declares (session iii): "In matters of faith and morals that enter into the edifice of Christian doctrine, that must be regarded as the true sense of Sacred Scripture which is held and has been held by Holy Mother Church, whose office it is to judge concerning the true sense and interpretation of the Holy Scriptures. And therefore no one is at liberty to interpret Holy Writ contrary to this sense, or even against the unanimous judgment of the Fathers."

Any sense of Scripture must be rejected that in any way brings the inspired authors into conflict with one another or is opposed to the teaching of the Church. Leo XIII, in his famous encyclical, *Providentissimus Deus,* gives two additional rules: (1) The literal sense must be retained unless necessity or a grave reason makes this impossible; (2) the allegorical sense is not to be despised when it depends on the literal sense and is supported by the authority of man.

What Has the Church Decided About Certain Passages of Scripture?

Dogmatic pronouncements have not been many. The Council of Trent listed the books of the Old and New Testaments that were accepted as authentic and canonical in the Church. It declared that the Vulgate, or St. Jerome's Latin translation, should be regarded as conforming to the original text (D. 785). This decree does not declare that the Vulgate is simply the best of all Biblical versions, but only that the Vulgate contains everything essential to salvation, and is not subject to error in matters of faith and morals.

The Council of Trent defined directly that St. Paul's Epistle to the Romans, v. 12, speaks certainly of original sin (D. 791). It decreed that the words of Jesus to Nicodemus: "Amen, amen, I say to you, unless a man be born again of water and the Holy Spirit he cannot enter the Kingdom of God," affirm the absolute necessity of Baptism. (D. 791 & 858) It declared that the words of the institution of the Eucharist must be understood in the literal and not the metaphorical sense (D. 874); that the words of John xx, 23, certainly affirm that the Church was given the power to forgive sins (D. 894); and that the passage in James v, 14, contains the promulgation of the sacrament of Extreme Unction (D. 908). The Vatican Council defined that Matt. xvi, 16, contains the words of Christ promising Peter the primacy, and that it was actually conferred in the text of John xxi, 15. This seems to be all the precisely defined Scriptural texts. (Cartechini, *Dall' Opinione al Domma,* p. 85)

How Does the Catholic Bible Differ from the Protestant?

There are such comparatively minor differences as the numbering of the Commandments and the Psalms (the Protestant Twenty-third Psalm is the Catholic Twenty-second; the Protestant version makes the First Commandment into two and then turns the Ninth and Tenth into one). Sometimes the phraseology is different (e.g., the Protestant "peace on earth, good will to men" is rendered "peace on earth to men of good will" in the Douay-Challoner). The important word *presbyter* is misleadingly given a literal translation in the King James version. In that version, too, "For Thine is the kingdom" is added to the Lord's Prayer, though it does not appear in any Catholic Bible. Luther added the word "alone" to St. Paul's sentence: "We are justified by faith." But the greatest differences are in the books included in the Old Testament.

Only the Catholic Bible contains, in the Old Testament, the books of Tobias, Judith, Wisdom, Baruch, Ecclesiasticus, and I and II Machabees. Only the Catholic Bible contains the following parts of Old Testament books: Esther x–xvi; Daniel iii, 24–90; Daniel xiii & xiv. Many non-Catholic Bibles now omit John vii, 53–viii, 11 (the story of the woman taken in adultery), or Luke xxii, 44–45 (the Bloody Sweat) as not belonging to the Scriptures.

Catholic Bibles in the Old Testament portions follow the Alexandrian canon, which included the books originally translated from the Hebrew into Greek, and which goes back to before 250 B.C. The Alexandrian canon was used by the Greek-speaking Jews of Alexandria, Asia Minor, and Italy. Of the 350 quotations from the Old Testament contained in the New, 300 are taken directly from the Septuagint, used by the Alexandrians. The writers of the first three centuries often quote or allude to them.

Chapter 8

The Heads of Catholic Doctrine

ALTHOUGH the Catholic dogmatic system may seem to be a lush jungle to anyone who opens a copy of Denziger's *Enchiridion Symbolorum*, the principal dogmas are not numerous and are easily learned, since none of them stands in isolation. The key dogmas determine all the rest. In the dogmatic theologies they are grouped according to seven tracts, besides the tract on revelation. They are: "God as One," "God as Triune," "God as Creator and Elevator," "The Incarnate Word," "Grace and Virtues," "The Sacraments," and "The Last Things."

"God as One" gives the arguments for the existence of God, and His attributes. "God as Triune" treats of the Trinity, Father, Son, and Holy Spirit. "God as Creator and Elevator" deals with the creation of the angels and the fall of some of them; the creation of the first human pair, their temptation by Satan and fall. "The Incarnate Word" examines the union of the Son of God, the Second Person in the Trinity, with human nature, and includes a subsidiary tract on the Redemption of the human race by Christ, the Blessed Mother of God, the saints, and relics. The Grace tract speaks of the helps God gives to man. The sacramental tracts treat of the seven sacraments and the grace they bestow. "The Last Things" treat of the Final Judgment, heaven, hell, and purgatory.

All Catholic dogmas converge in the great central doctrine, that of the Incarnation and Redemption. This tremendous event looks backward to the beginning of the human race, and takes in all the centuries that saw the gradual ripening of the Mosaic revelation. It looks forward in time to the activity of the Church in her saving mission for all future ages, and it looks beyond time to the Last Things of men.

All the dogmas of Catholic faith are summarized in the short Apostles' Creed, which the Catholic child learns in his catechism lesson.

What Is the Trinity?

This is the most sublime of Christian mysteries, since it reveals to us the intimate life of God, which we could never have guessed existed were it not for revelation, and cannot understand even after it has been revealed. St. Thomas writes: "He who tries to prove the Trinity of Persons in God by natural reason doubly derogates from faith: (1) As regards the dignity of faith, which consists in having as its object invisible things, which excludes the light of human reason. . . . (2) as regards the good of drawing others to faith. For when someone tries to prove faith by means of arguments that are not cogent he invites the derision of unbelievers." (*Summa*, I, q. 32, art. 1)

Nevertheless, no repugnance can be proved to exist in the dogma of the Trinity when rightly expounded. The Trinity is expressed in these terms: God is *absolutely* one in nature or essence, and *relatively* three in Persons (Father, Son, and Holy Spirit), who are really distinct from each other but are identical with the Divine Substance. (Parente, *Dictionary of Dogmatic Theology*, art. "Trinity") We say that God is one under the aspect of nature, and triune under the aspect of Persons. Now any being can be one under some aspect, and many under another aspect. Thus in man there are two substances, a spiritual substance, or soul, and a material substance, or body, and yet there is but one person. In order to prove that a contradiction exists in this mystery one must show that there is no distinction, even virtual, between a nature and a person. But this is impossible.

The Trinity is conceived in this wise:

God the Father is God, knowing Himself.

God the Son is the Word of the Father, or the expression of God's knowledge of Himself.

God the Holy Spirit is the result of God's love for Himself. (Trese, *God, Man, and God-Man*, p. 28)

The Son is generated by the Father, in somewhat the same way as the intellect generates a word. The Holy Spirit proceeds from the Father and the Son, not by generation, but after the manner of will, as the love that exists between Both.

The Three Persons are perfectly equal. We must not think of God the Father as coming first and God the Son a little later and God the Holy Spirit last. All three are co-eternal. We think of God the Father as creating, although all Three Persons create, since they are all three the same God. To the Holy Spirit we appropriate the work of sanctification. To the Son, who alone became incarnate, we appropriate the work of Redemption. And yet, since they have all the same divine substance, what one does all do.

Who Are the Angels?

God first created the angels. Angels are pure spirits, absolutely without bodies, who play an important part in sacred history. They are mentioned in innumerable places in Scripture. They were created in what might be termed a state of progress to the goal of the face-to-face or Beatific Vision of God, that is, they were tried by God before they were admitted to their end. Some of them fell through pride, expressed in an act of undetermined nature. These we call demons, devils, or by the collective name, Satan. Hell, a place of eternal punishment, was created when the devils fell. By their deliberate and fully conscious rejection of God their wills were fixed against God forever. The angels who persevered were admitted to the presence of God and became His servants (angel means messenger).

Satan, in the guise of a serpent, successfully tempted Adam and Eve, the first parents of the present human race, and as a result they lost their supernatural and preternatural gifts, which otherwise they would have transmitted to their descendants.

As regards the good angels, it is certain that every human being has a guardian angel to save him from undue danger, beyond the divine will.

Does the Catholic Church Believe in Diabolical Possession?

The existence of demoniacal possession, which means that a devil enters into the body of a person and takes control of his physical activities—speech, movements, and actions—is certain Catholic teaching, being plainly mentioned in the Gospels. In the ritual of the Church there is a special ceremony for the purpose of casting out a devil who has taken possession of man. This is called exorcism. The office of exorcist belongs to every priest, but it may not be officially exercised except with special permission from the Bishop, and then only after careful investigation has established that it is not a case of simple mental illness. Theologians hold that demoniacal possession is probably frequent in primitive regions but is not common today in civilized countries, where the devil tries subtler means of tormenting man. Still, every so often one reads of a priest performing the office of exorcist, even in the United States.

God allows demoniacal temptation and possession as He allows other trials, to punish or purify or try man, or for our instruction.

What Is Catholic Teaching on the Evolution of Man?

What may be called free-lance Catholic writers sometimes lead the reader to think that the Catholic view on the evolution of man's body is more liberal than it is. As a matter of fact all the authors of the dogmatic manuals I have seen—Herve, Tanquerey, Lercher, Hugon, et al.—take a dim view of the question. The evolution of man may not be taught in the Catholic theological schools; it may only be investigated. Pius XII makes this clear in his encyclical, *Humani Generis:*

"The teaching authority of the Church does not forbid that, in conformity with the present state of human sciences and sacred theology, research and discussions on the part of men experienced in both fields take place with regard to the doctrine of evolution insofar as it inquires into the origin of the human body as coming from pre-existent and living matter—for Catholic faith obliges us to hold that souls are immediately created by God. But this must be done in such a way that the reasons for both opinions, that is, those favorable and those unfavorable to evolution, be weighed and judged with the necessary seriousness, moderation, and measure, and provided that all are prepared to submit to the judgment of the Church, to whom Christ has given the mission of interpreting authentically Sacred Scripture and of defending dogmas of faith." (Paulist Press translation, p. 19)

According to the same encyclical, Catholics may not teach that the present human race descended from more than one human pair, for otherwise the dogma of original sin would be endangered. The theory of man's bodily evolution is hard to reconcile with the Scholastic doctrine of the rational soul as the form of the human body and with the Genesiac account and Catholic tradition, to say nothing of the recent discoveries of science.

Our first parents, Adam and Eve, were constituted in a state of integral nature, that is, they were immune from ignorance (relative to what they needed to know), pain, and death. Their lower natures would not have rebelled against the higher. They were created in a state of sanctity and righteousness, in which they could with difficulty sin.

But our first parents sinned by gravely transgressing a command of God. They thus lost for themselves and for their posterity the preternatural gifts of immunity from suffering and death, and the supernatural gift of sanctifying grace, which is a quality given to the soul that makes it especially pleasing to God.

By his sin, Adam transmitted to his descendants a nature deprived of this sanctifying grace. As a consequence, and in this particular sense, we are born hateful to God and in a state of spiritual death. This is what is called original sin, which all men contract with the sole exception of the Mother of Christ, by virtue of a special privilege.

Although Baptism restores to us the supernatural gift of sanctifying grace and restores us to the friendship of God, it does not restore the preternatural gifts, such as freedom from suffering and death. This transmission of original sin, which is not voluntary in us but exists only as a privation of good things, is not unjust. Our misfortune is often compared by theologians to that of the children of a man who culpably neglected to provide for his family. The man was at fault, the children were not. Nevertheless, their poverty is not unjust, since wealth was not due to them.

After Adam, man was inclined to sin; he fell away from the pure worship of God. Heaven, which is the place of union with God, was debarred to him, although unless he died in mortal sin he would not have gone to hell. The way was set for the Incarnation of the Son of God. All the two-thousand-year history of the Chosen People of God, from Abraham to Christ, was by way of preparing the world for that event. In Christ all the prophecies of Jeremias and Isaias converged.

What Is the Incarnation?

The Incarnation of the Second Person of the Trinity is the mysterious union (called Hypostatic) of the divine nature and of the human nature in the Person of the Word. The Incarnate Word is Jesus Christ, true God and true Man.

Jesus Christ had two powers of saying *I:* He could say *"I existed with the Father from all eternity,"* and *"I was born in a stable in Bethlehem."* He had a human soul and a human will and a human operation and a human nature. But He had only one Person, His personality as the Son of God, eternally existing in the Trinity. There is in Christ only one Person (the Word) because there is in Him only one existence, that of the Word. But there are two natures, the divine and the human, that are distinct.

The Incarnation is another mystery of faith that is impervious to human reason, but it can be shown to be not repugnant. The Divine Word did not lay aside His Divine Nature, but the human nature He united to Himself will last forever. Christ as a man possessed an infused knowledge, by which He knew things by means of ideas or images immediately infused by God. He always enjoyed the vision of His Father. He also possessed, like other men, an experimental knowledge, which enabled Him to advance in wisdom. He was sinless and holy and possessed complete liberty. He could suffer and feel pain and sadness but assumed a perfect, entire, and well-ordered human body, as was suitable to His condition.

Why Did God Become Incarnate?

Man, a finite creature, can never give God back what he takes away by sin. Sin is in a manner infinite, since it denies the infinite dignity of God. Only a Man-God could repair the offense done to God. If God chose to demand reparation according to strict justice, only someone capable of dying and offering an infinite reparation could meet this need. No mere creature could ever offer God infinite satisfaction. But if a man has a divine personality all his acts are of infinite value, for acts belong to the person. The Incarnation was not strictly necessary, because God could have repaired in various other ways the ruin caused by Adam's sin. He could have annihilated the human race or reduced it to the natural order. Or He could have given man a gratuitous pardon. But if He chose to demand perfect satisfaction the Incarnation was necessary.

Because He was also God, the least of Christ's sufferings was sufficient to satisfy for man's sin; but Jesus suffered a most cruel death on the Cross, in obedience to the command to die He received from His Father (Phil. ii, 8), and thus satisfied superabundantly for all the sins of the human race, whether original or actual.

This does not mean, however, that we need do nothing on our part to be restored to God's grace. It still is necessary for each one of us, individually, to apply to himself the merits of Christ's atoning sacrifice.

Who Is the Mother of God?

That Mary, the Mother of Christ, is the Mother of God follows from the fact that Christ is a Divine Person, and generation terminates in the Person, not the Divine Nature, or the human nature. The Divine Person of Christ could both say "I am God" and "I am Man." Therefore, unless we are willing to deny that Christ is divine, we must admit that His Mother is the Mother of God.

The dignity of the Mother of God far surpasses all other dignities, with the exception of the Hypostatic Union. For the Virgin, by contributing the matter of Christ's body, and by voluntarily conceiving, bearing, and nurturing it, was, as it were, the instrumental cause of the Hypostatic Union and a co-operator of the Divine Persons in the great work of the Incarnation. Wherefore, says St. Thomas, "the Blessed Virgin, by the fact that she is the Mother of God, has in a way an infinite dignity, owing to the infinite Good that is God." (*Summa*, III, q. 25, art. 6)

A mother is not just the mother of her child's physical body; she is the mother of all of him. There would have been no reason for God's becoming incarnate at all unless He was to have a real mother, whom He could love and honor. The Word assumed human nature in all its relations, foremost of which is that between mother and child. That is why Catholics love and honor her. They do not pay her divine honors, but they accord her a veneration that stands in a special place above that given to the saints. This is called the cultus of hyperdulia.

It is divine and Catholic doctrine that Mary came into the world exempt from original sin and never committed the slightest sin. She always remained a virgin and upon her death was assumed bodily into heaven. Because of her eminent dignity she is honored as the queen of men and angels and as the mother of all Christians in the supernatural order, for Mary is the Mother of Jesus, who became our Brother.

It is Catholic doctrine—that is, not proposed formally as the Word of God but expressly taught in the whole Church—that the Virgin intercedes for us in heaven, and that her intercession is so universal that every grace passes through her hands. The mediation of all the saints is subordinate to hers. The mediation of Mary is, of course, absolutely subordinate to God, so that whatever mercy is found in Mary must be attributed to the divine bounty. The intercession of the Virgin, which has value even in virtue of Mary's own merits, rests ultimately on the merits of Christ, by grace of which she was immaculate, chosen as the Mother of God, and perfectly sanctified. (Herve, *Manuale Theologiae Dogmaticae*, II, N. 661)

The Church, of course, would never permit anything resembling divine honors to be paid to Mary. "The smallest of our children, the simplest of our good women," says the author of the "Mariolatrie" article in *Dictionnaire apologétique*, col. 325–326, "would rebel at the mere idea of putting on the same footing the divine cultus of the Holy Eucharist, where God Himself is present, with the cultus of the Blessed Virgin." Exaggerations of the Marian cultus have, in fact, been rare. Theodore Studites, in the ninth century, rebuked the monk Theoctistos, who said that Mary "existed before time." (*Ibid.*, col. 328) An extravagant book about Mary's place of honor was placed on the Index in 1758, and more recently the Church condemned the formula, "Queen of the Sacred Heart," because it implied, or seemed to imply, an inferior position of Christ. The Church forbids the Infant Jesus to be placed side by side with Mary in images; He must always be in her arms. (*Ibid.*)

The great centers of Marian devotion—Lourdes, LaSalette, Fatima, Our Lady of Guadalupe—which owed their origin to apparitions of the Virgin, had to fight their way to acceptance by Church authorities for many years before they were finally approved.

Far from being a corruption, Catholic honors to Mary are but the marvelous flower of the dogma of the Incarnation, which they render tangible and vital.

What Is the Cultus of the Saints and Images?

As devotion to Mary is a natural result of the Incarnation, whereby the Son of God sanctified humanity by assuming it, so also, in a lesser degree, is the cultus of the saints, of images, and of the relics of the saints. The saints are heroes of God, and, because of the heroic acts whereby they won eminence on earth and the glory that they share in heaven, they reflect some of the supernatural eminence of Christ, and hence ought to be acknowledged with a special reverence, which is however below that given to Mary, and of course infinitely below that given to God. Because of the love the saints have for us and the power they enjoy with God they are ready to obtain many benefits for us. This devotion is also justified by the veneration that was paid to the angels and to holy men in Sacred Scripture. (Job xliii, 8; Acts viii, 60; Rom. xv, 30, etc.)

The cultus of images and the relics of the saints stands in a class by itself. This is a relative honor; that is, it does not rest in these objects themselves, but goes on to the saints with whom they were associated. The sentimental cherishing of a picture, of a lock of hair of a loved one, and of historical objects, such as those in Mount Vernon, are apt parallels.

What Is Grace?

Nothing is more distinctive of the Christian economy than the doctrine of grace. Grace has several meanings in Catholic theology, but in general it signifies a special benevolence or favor of God—something not due to man's nature.

Actual grace is a supernatural help, whereby God illuminates the intellect and assists the will to elicit a supernatural act, such as that of faith or charity. It is of divine faith that, without a truly supernatural grace of illumination and inspiration, fallen man is not even physically able to elicit supernatural acts that prepare him to receive the benefit of the merits of Jesus Christ, which is that of adoption into the family of God. Even for the beginning of faith, even for the desire to accomplish any supernatural work, such as an act of divine faith, God's grace is necessary. Only a supernatural help enables us to perform a supernatural act. An act of faith in God or an act of love of God is as supernatural for us as thinking would be for a horse; it enables us to act on a divine level. The first stirrings of grace in ourselves are so much the work of God that, as the common doctrine holds, first actual grace is not obtained merely by human prayers or by an ordinary natural disposition, but by a free gift.

Moreover, without the help of grace, fallen man is practically unable to continue long to observe the whole natural law and overcome serious temptations for any great length of time, although he can perform some morally good acts of the easier sort, such as love of parents or simple philanthropy.

The Catholic Church teaches that God gives sufficient graces for their salvation to all the just, all common sinners, all hardened sinners, and all adult infidels. God permits men to be blinded and hardened in sin by their abuse or contempt of grace, but He does not abandon them before He is first abandoned by them. After the first promptings of grace, man must co-operate with God by the exercise of his own will. God does most of the work, but man must help. This co-operative action of man is likened to the walking of an invalid while supported by the arms and shoulders of his nurse. The nurse helps raise and support the man, but he or she cannot help him to walk if he insists on remaining a dead weight, without using any of his muscles.

Besides actual grace, there is what is called habitual grace, which makes man pleasing to God. The Church teaches that justification, whereby we are made adoptive sons of God, does not consist in the mere legal imputation of the merits of Christ, which simply declares us His adopted sons, but in the infusion of grace, which transforms the soul and truly blots out sins.

"This participation of the divine nature," says Tanquerey (*Brevior*, NN. 908–909), "is a special and supernatural assimilation to God, far transcending the natural similarity to Him that is in all creatures, or the similarity of image, which is imprinted on the human mind. . . . For by the assimilation of grace we are made capable of immediately seeing God, without any created medium . . . and we are already called 'partakers of the divine nature.' (II Pet. i, 4)

"Hence the soul adorned by grace possesses a wonderful beauty. It is resplendent with divine glory and brightness, somewhat as a globe of purest crystal shines and gleams in the light of the sun. Perfect order begins to reign in the faculties, and the inferior powers are subject to the will, and the reason and the will are subject to God."

This grace of justification can be lost, and in fact is lost, by every serious sin. This grace consists of two elements, the indwelling of the Divine Trinity in the soul of every just man, which is called "uncreated grace," and created grace, which is a quality that so raises the soul above its level that it can reflect the image of the Creator. This grace is the means whereby man can come as close to God as any mere creature possibly may.

Besides this habitual grace, the just man has infused virtues. These are the theological virtues of faith, hope, and charity, whereby he immediately reaches God on this earth, and the four moral virtues of justice, prudence, fortitude, and temperance, which regulate all moral life. These infused virtues incline man to exercise supernatural acts, but they do not necessarily confer an ease of performing them, as do habits acquired by practice. Neither do they demand the exercise of reason or free will. They inhere in the baby at Baptism and in the sleeping man, since one does not cease to be virtuous because his faculties are undeveloped or suspended. The infused moral virtues, which dispose man to receive the guidance of the reason as elevated by the theological virtues of faith, hope, and charity, are more perfect than the acquired moral virtues, which dispose him to follow the guidance of the unaided natural reason.

Grace, however, ordinarily never destroys nature; it builds upon it. The substratum of the supernatural life, in Catholic theology, is always human nature considered in itself and in its moral faculties, reason, will, and the appetites. The natural, acquired virtues of prudence, justice, fortitude, and temperance prepare and perfect man for the infused virtues of that name; and the supernatural, infused virtues of justice, temperance, fortitude, and prudence in their turn bend our wills to act in a manner consistent with the three theological virtues of faith, hope, and charity, which immediately adjust us to God. By the help of this twofold organism of grace and nature we act and live a perfect and virtuous life, as worthy brothers of Christ and sons of God.

Chapter 9

How It All Ends

WE COME NOW to the culmination of every Catholic manual or summation of dogmatic theology, the tract on the Last Things of man and the world. It explains where and how each human being ends, according to the degree in which he has co-operated with God's grace.

The Catholic Church teaches that death ends man's trial on earth. After the soul has crossed the barrier of the body there is no more opportunity to gain merit; neither will it deserve increased punishment for anything it does henceforth. Time, in a way, comes to an end, for the soul no longer makes decisions affecting its salvation. It is either confirmed in grace or frozen in sin.

At death every soul is judged, and assigned its permanent fate. Those of the just in whom no punishment remains to be paid after their death will immediately possess the intuitive vision of God and love Him with a love that brings happiness unimaginable on earth. This vision is clear and intuitive—not seen through the medium of any image or idea—but in His very Essence. God is not seen through an object that is first known, but is immediately *united* to the blessed intellect, united to it as the thing that is immediately and directly known.

It is this possession of God, a possession that is complete but never comprehensive, since no creature can exhaust an Infinite Being, that constitutes the end for which we were made. Besides this all-embracing essential happiness there are many accidental sources of happiness, such as infused knowledge, reunion with friends, and, after the general resurrection, the glories of body surpassingly beautiful that can move from place to place at the mere inclination of the soul, can penetrate other bodies without hurt, and is beyond reach of suffering.

Opposite to heaven is hell, a place and state of punishment that never ends. Hell corresponds in inverse ratio to heaven. Just as in heaven the essential happiness is the possession of God, so in hell the essential misery is the pain of loss—the loss of God. As in heaven there are the delights of sense—those delights, namely, that have nothing to do with the functions of nourishment and reproduction, which will cease after death—so in hell there are the pains of sense, the principal of which is the burning of a preternatural fire that never gives light and never is extinguished. As in heaven not all are equal, but some will be higher than others, according to the merits they have gained by co-operating with God's grace on earth, so in hell there are gradations of punishment according to wickedness.

As heaven contains, or will contain sooner or later, all those who have died in the friendship of God, so hell contains all those who have perished in unforgiven mortal sin, which robs the soul of its spiritual life. It is supremely probable, as several theologians think, that God would not allow a sinner to go to hell for an isolated mortal sin, especially one of frailty, but that only inveterate sinners go there. (*Dictionnaire de la théologie catholique,* art. "Enfer," col. 116)

It is Catholic teaching that God does not properly send anyone to hell. The true, direct, efficient cause of this terrible punishment is the sinner himself. The sinner digs his own pit. God is only the indirect efficient cause, as the Author of nature with its essential laws. (*Ibid.*, col. 115) God's justice in hell is not a personal vengeance; He always pardons, with that pardon which continues to will good; but He gives only possible good; the damned never more will wish grace, and thus can never receive it. (*Ibid.*, col. 116) It follows that the blessed in heaven do not pity the damned, for such pity would be misplaced. The damned are not simply unhappy, they are miserable. God has no mercy on the lost, because they do not wish mercy. We shall understand that perfectly only in the infinite light of eternity.

Sin, say all the theologians, is an evil, an offense to the Infinite Being, and therefore it must be in some manner truly infinite, both in itself and its punishment. The sinner voluntarily turns away from God, hence we have the pain of loss; the sinner voluntarily turns to creatures, hence he is punished by creatures through the pain of sense. Sin has no other point of view; it is evil, disorder. Disorder can never of itself become order. Hell is eternal, so the Church teaches as of divine faith, according to the Council of Constantinople (553).

Adjacent to hell, and sometimes classified with it, is Limbo, the Limbo of the Children. Christ Himself refers by various names and figures to the place or state that Catholic tradition calls the Limbo of the Fathers, where the just of the Old Testament went before the Redemption opened the gates of heaven (e.g., Matt. viii, 11; Luke xvi, 22. It is also mentioned in Eph. iv, 9, and I Pet. iii, 18–20). The New Testament contains no definite statement regarding the eternal lot of those who die in original sin alone, but the absolute necessity of Baptism for heaven demands a place where children go who are not regenerated with the saving waters. It is a place of natural happiness, without the vision of God but also without sorrow or pain. We shall discuss this further, under Baptism.

It is the common feeling of Catholics, based on the nature of most Christians, that few are prepared for immediate entrance into heaven, though they do not deserve eternal punishment at the moment of death. For them purgatory awaits, a place and state in which the souls of the just who die with a debt of temporal punishment for sins forgiven suffer until all their debts have been paid. The existence of purgatory is of divine faith, being proved clearly from II Machabees xii, 46: "It is therefore a holy and wholesome thought to pray for the dead, that they may be loosed from sins." It is also proved from both Jewish and Christian tradition and is at least strongly hinted at in the words of Christ in Matthew xii, 32: "Whoever speaks against the Holy Spirit, it will not be forgiven him, either in this world or in the world to come." It is here supposed that certain sins can be forgiven in the future life; and, since it is certain that mortal sins are not forgiven after death, the reference must be to lesser or venial sins, or else to the punishment due for mortal sin already forgiven.

The doctrine of purgatory is the foundation for the granting of indulgences for good works, usually prayers, by which something is remitted of the punishment due in purgatory for sins committed on earth. Indulgences do not forgive sin; they only abate a part of the punishment for sin, whether it is venial sin, which does not merit eternal death, or mortal sin, which deserves hell, but which has been forgiven by repentance and the sacrament of Penance.

The Church has defined nothing about the punishments of purgatory. It is certain that the souls detained there know that they are saved and can no longer sin. They suffer from being deprived temporarily of the Beatific Vision. It is commonly admitted in the Western part of the Church that the suffering souls are tormented by a real fire, at least to the extent of being fettered by it.

The world will not last forever, but at some undetermined time there will be a universal consummation, marked by a radical change in the earth and heavens and by a general resurrection of all the dead. The Fourth Lateran Council declared it of faith that all men will rise again with the bodies they now bear. This is proved from several passages in the Old and the New Testaments (e.g., Dan. xii, 2; Matt. v, 29–30; John v, 29; Acts xvii, 31–32).

At the general resurrection there will also take place a Universal Judgment, at which Christ will, in a very brief moment, pronounce judgment on all men, not to declare their eternal fate, which is decided for each human being at the particular judgment, but to manifest His justice to all. (Matt. xxv, 31–46; II Cor. v, 10)

And so we come to the end of this very brief outline of the wonderful structure called dogmatic theology. Whether a dogma is of divine faith, or is called Catholic doctrine; whether a proposition is called theologically certain, or safe, or common, or simply probable, it is never proposed without arguments, drawn from the ecclesiastical Magisterium, from Scripture, from Tradition, and from reason.

I repeat what I have said earlier: all dogmas cohere in a

marvelous unity; even free opinions relate to what has been taught or can be found in Scripture or Tradition. Nothing is entirely new, except in our manner of understanding it. Catholic dogmatic and moral theology, together with Scholastic philosophy, is unique in the thought systems of the world.

Chapter 10

What Is Moral Theology?

MORAL THEOLOGY in the Catholic Church is sometimes called practical theology; it is the reduction to practice of the demands made by God on men. It is for practical theology that dogmatic theology exists. Yet neither dogmatic nor moral theology is the ultimate authority in the Church. That rests alone with the Magisterium, the teaching office of Pope and Bishops united with him.

The moral theologies usually studied in seminaries fall into three or four parts. The first part will deal with the principles of moral life—human and divine law, conscience and responsibility, and the nature and classification of sin. The second part will apply the principles of moral science to each of the Commandments of the Decalogue. A third part will treat of the sacraments and the rules for their vail or lawful reception. Treated separately is a section on the penalties the Church employs to enforce her law when she deems this advisable.

No one will understand moral theology if he takes its precepts as a set of rules for a club. There are numerous laws of the Church that bind only the clergy. There are other laws that bind Catholics but not others of the baptized. There are still others that are considered as having obligatory force also for baptized non-Catholics, whether they realize it or not; but not for the unbaptized.

Most of the applications of moral science are not drawn from the human law of the Church but from divine law and extend to all men, as being of the natural or divine law. Ethics, for example, which is a branch of philosophy, is not the exclusive concern of Catholics or the nonconcern of those who are not Catholics. Catholic teaching must support right ethics, but one does not exempt oneself from its law by remaining outside the Catholic Church.

Similarly, although critics of the Church often speak of a "Catholic code of sex morality" or the "discipline of the Church in regard to birth control," such terms are not accurate. The laws governing the use of sex rest on all alike. Although a marriage may be invalid for a Catholic where it would be valid for a non-Catholic, once a marriage is valid it is subject to the universal rules of indissolubility established by the natural law, to which exception can be made only by the divine law, in the interests of the Faith.

The science that treats of the moral life teaches that no one may persuade another to do what is objectively a sin for him, even though subjectively, in his conscience, he is not aware of sin and hence does not incur guilt. Thus in itself it would not be a sin for a Catholic employer to impose Sunday work on the nonbaptized, but it would be wrong to demand this without necessity of the baptized non-Catholic, though the non-Catholic might see nothing wrong in violating the Sunday rest. The moral law is independent of the individual conscience.

What Determines Morality?

First of all, there must be a human act, one performed with knowledge, will, and freedom. Acts done in a state of semisleep, mental illness, fear, extreme passion, or ignorance are not imputable as good or bad in themselves, although, as in the case of drunkenness or willful ignorance, a man may be responsible for putting himself in a position of irresponsibility.

But the ultimate rule for the rightness or wrongness of every human act is always the eternal law of God, who made man for Himself. The immediate rule is the human mind, insofar as it recognizes the eternal law and applies it to its actions. It is by no means necessary for a person to be thinking particularly about the law of God. It is enough if he sees that his act agrees with, or does not agree with, right reason as he knows it. It follows that an act can be subjectively good while being bad in itself. A Robin Hood who steals from the rich to give to the poor does not incur the guilt of theft if he sees nothing wrong with that. It is good as far as he is concerned. But he has the duty to enlighten his conscience the moment he suspects he is not following right reason in this business.

Whether an act will agree with right reason or not depends on three things: the object, the circumstances, and the end.

The object is what the action is about. The object of theft is taking another's property; of murder, taking innocent life. An object is called good if it is worthy of a rational creature, as to adore God or give alms; it is called bad if it is unworthy of human nature, as to lie, blaspheme, or steal; it is called indifferent if it is something, like eating, walking, writing, which in itself is neither worthy nor unworthy of rational nature.

Some objects are evil absolutely and independently of any condition, because they are so repugnant to rational nature that not even God could change them. One example is a lie, though this is not usually a mortal sin.

No act whose object is essentially bad can become good by virtue of end or circumstances. Not even God could command anyone to tell the least lie. But often accidental conditions may take away the evil of an act not wicked in itself. Thus, within limits, custom may make a mode of woman's dress cease to be immodest. The stealing by a child from its parents is usually less grievous than a stranger's stealing, because parents are less unwilling as to the amount taken by their children. Conversely, the increased destruction of modern warfare makes wars unjustified that in an earlier age might be justified.

In practice there is no such thing as an utterly indifferent act. Everything not evil in its object, end, or circumstances can be referred to God and therefore become good.

Whence Are Moral Rules Drawn?

The ultimate sources are divine revelation and human reason judging the conformity of a thing with man's nature. The infallible Magisterium—Popes, e.g., in addresses to medical conventions, in condemning certain propositions, in encyclicals; councils of the Church, the responses of the Roman congregations—sometimes give guide lines for interpreting reason or revelation. But whenever there is no agreement among weighty moral theologians on a point of morals the Church Teaching does not often intervene. Moral decisions are comparatively few. About 150 moral propositions have been condemned by the Popes.

The chief written document from which truths of the moral order are drawn is Scripture, chiefly the New Testament. Thus the Catholic teaching about the sinfulness of birth control is taken from, or confirmed by, two chief Biblical texts, Genesis xxxviii, 10, and Romans i, 27. But even if it were not contained in Scripture it would be condemned by reason of the principles of the natural law.

Catholic tradition is an important guide to moral teaching. Thus the Council of Guarmacien in the Middle Ages; the bull of Sixtus V, *Effrenatam* (October 29, 1588); some seven answers of the Roman Congregations, ranging in time from 1851 to 1918; and the solemn warning of Pius XI in the encyclical, *Casti Connubii,* issued December 31, 1930, that confessors must "not allow the faithful to be misled in regard to this most grave law of God," all go to establish the constant tradition of the Church against birth control.

We find evidence of the practice of birth control from the earliest times by some Catholics. Mention of it as a sin repented of and forgiven is found in the *Philosophumena* (Kirch, *Enchiridion Fontium Historiae Ecclesiasticae Antiquae,* N. 233, 6) of St. Hippolyte of Rome, who died in 235. We find it condemned in St. Augustine, we find it alluded to and condemned in the *Parson's Tale* of Chaucer. Nowhere do we find it approved. Therefore we must conclude, according to the rule that fact cannot contradict fact in Christian doctrine (called the analogy of faith), that birth control is condemned by the infallible tradition of the Church, and it would have been condemned even without an encyclical from Pius XI.

As in dogmatic theology, the universal opinion of the Fathers and theologians in any age is enough to establish certainty in moral science. Even one Father or theologian of great name could make a judgment probable. The common opinion of almost all moral theologians yields such a weight of testimony that it would be rash to resist them. On the other hand, the authority of even many theologians, if other competent theologians are opposed, has no greater power to create faith than the proof afforded by their arguments. (Noldin, *Summa Theologiae Moralis,* I, N. 10)

Moralists are not confined to Scripture and Tradition in solving moral questions. They may make extensive use of psychology, sociology, political economy, jurisprudence, and the history of morals. They can, of course, conclude nothing against the analogy of faith, or what does not square with the traditional teaching of the Church, but even revealed truths must be reasonably proposed, and authority far from being a hindrance in the application of these sciences is a great help.

The Holy Office in Rome has the right of making definitions in all cases affecting heresy, schism, apostasy, magic, and the abuse of the sacraments. Its doctrinal responses enjoy great authority, especially since they are always approved by the Sovereign Pontiff, although most often this approbation is routine and does not render these decrees infallible. (Tanquerey, *Brevior,* II, N. 10)

The general rule of moral doctrine, which sums up all particular rules, is this: human acts must be proportionate to their Last End, which is God. I repeat: man learns the will of God not only from revelation, but also by reasoning on what is consistent with his nature.

Does Catholicity Admit Progress in Moral Science?

If the morality of an act were determined only by its object, its morality would be as changeless as the object. But, since circumstances and ends often have a great deal to do with a moral act, morality may sometimes *seem* to change according to circumstances. The principles of morality, however, never change.

An example of this seeming change is the different attitude toward interest now and in medieval times. At that time all profit taken from a loan was unjust and was called usury. In this prohibition there was something changeless, the natural law that forbids us to demand something more than what was given. Injustice is always a sin.

Formerly conditions were not such that money could be easily exchanged for fruitful things or used for business profit. But now, on account of the great opportunities offered for investment, this is so; money has become fruitful. But these changed conditions do not falsify the affirmation of Benedict XIV, when in 1745 he condemned usury: "That all gain derived from a loan precisely as a loan is forbidden by every law, natural, divine, and ecclesiastical, was and is the constant doctrine of the Catholic Church."

Also, moral, like dogmatic, theology has its periods of growth and decline. It can never lead the Church into error, but in some ages it is developed better than in others. Moral science may be enriched with new data and the intellects of its scientists whetted by conflict with new errors and wrestling with new problems.

War and warfare, which used to be handled in a page of simple rules in some major manuals of theology, like Noldin's, now demand greater attention from theologians because of the frightening complexities of modern cold war and cold peace, and above all the terrific destruction of atomic and hydrogen weapons.

Man-made laws, even those passed by the Church, can be abrogated and modified, and be liberalized in their application. An example is the Church law of fast, which, on account of modern conditions, is not observed so strictly as in former times, by permission of the Church itself.

Often we find people, who cannot discern the perfectly clear principles of moral science, thinking that the moral law changes, when only the subject matter of the law changes. Take the principle of the double effect, which is not at all complex. This is resolved into two principles, the first of which says that an evil effect, willed or intended only in its cause, is imputable to the one who places the cause only if he foresaw the evil that would follow, could avoid placing the cause, and did not need to prevent the effect.

The second principle says that to do a thing that is good or indifferent in itself, from which two effects follow, one good, the other bad, can be justified and made good for a proportionate reason, provided the bad effect is not used as a means to achieve the good effect.

A general in a just war may bomb a munitions plant, even though he knows that many innocent people will be killed. A surgeon may excise a Fallopian tube, when there is danger to the mother's life in delay, even though he knows that an inviable child will thus perish. But he may by no means kill the child in a difficult delivery in order to save the mother's life, for this would be performing an intrinsically evil act. In the former case, the child is not killed, but simply allowed to die. No one is obliged to give his own life for another unless he has a duty to do this by virtue of a contract. On the other hand, no one may take innocent life to save no matter how many other innocent lives. What is evil by reason of its object always remains evil. If we could effect the death of a child in the womb in order to save the mother's life, so could we kill a person infected with a dangerously contagious disease in order to save other lives.

It used to be taught by some Catholic moralists that the removal of the Fallopian tube in an ectopic pregnancy was unlawful. The reason was not any misunderstanding of principle, but simply the acceptance of what seemed a safe scientific theory, that the tube in ectopic pregnancies was not diseased, and that the danger to the mother's life was caused only by the child. In that case it would never be lawful to remove the tube, for that would be killing the child to save the mother. But if, as modern medical opinion holds, the Fallopian tube is diseased in such cases, then the tube may be removed if this is immediately necessary to save the life of the mother, since it is always right to remove diseased parts of the body, even though incidentally some other person may suffer.

The point in this illustration is that circumstances, or the state of medical science, may change; moral principles never change. As I have repeatedly said, even the least lie could not be told—not if it were necessary to save the world. The end or the circumstances justify an act only if its object is not in itself evil. One who grasps this fact will have no difficulty with the moral science of Catholicity, and will not accuse it of sacrificing principle to expediency, or on the other hand of heartlessly sticking to rote and rule.

Chapter 11

What Is Law?

CATHOLICITY, since it is a religion of reason, must also be a religion of law. We have already seen the definition of law in the discussion of ethics.

Since God has the supreme care of the world, all law comes eventually from God, and unless a human law is consistent in some way with His reason and will it is no law. Here we come to a treatment of that law, which to ignore would make moral science meaningless. I mean the natural law.

The natural law is engraved on all hearts, and by force of human reason directs what is good and forbids what is wrong. (Rom. ii, 14–16; Vatican Council, session iii, cap. 2 on Revelation)

A great deal of confusion has existed about the natural law. Only recently a judge of a federal circuit court and a governor of a Southern state appealed to the fact that birds of different varieties flock together but do not congregate with birds of a different feather, as proof that racial dissegregation is against the natural law. People sometimes point to the cutting of the hair, the damming of rivers, etc., as proof that we are always doing something "against nature."

I repeat: the natural law has absolutely nothing to do with what biologists or physicists call "nature." It applies only to men. Animals are directed by the eternal law, which for them is simply God's providence. The natural law is simply the obligation imposed on men by the mere fact that they are men to act consistently with their nature. It takes in all the acts that human reason can see must be done, or not done, in view of man's relation to God, his neighbor, and himself.

This rule of conduct is called *natural* because it includes only those precepts that are founded on the nature of things and can be inferred by the natural light of reason. Parallels can be found in everyday life. One who has been employed for even a short time will know certain things that his employer expects of him, without being told. He will know that he must come to work on time and give a fair day's performance for a fair day's wages. He will take it for granted that his employer's property must be handled as the employer would wish it. All this could be called the natural law of business.

The positive law of an employer-employee relationship would include everything else that the employee could not be presumed to know, but must be told, such as the hours of work.

The natural law is an extension of the office or workshop to the whole of life. It commands what is good by its nature and necessary for the end of creation, and forbids everything that is bad by its nature and obstructs the end of creation.

Let us return to the case of birth control. Sometimes certain species of animals occasionally get sexual gratification out of the normal course of nature. This is not against the natural law. Anything that a beast does is natural for him.

In man, however, the same act is against the natural law, because it is against what his reason could tell him is right conduct for propagating the human race. The sex drive, like the hunger drive, was obviously implanted in man for a purpose, that of propagating the race within a stable union of man and wife for the rearing of children. If used contrary to that design, it is known to be a violation of God's will as learned from nature.

Whatever is against reason is against the natural law, even though the act itself be natural. Thus simple fornication, which involves no unnatural act, is contrary to natural law because it defies the rules natural reason gives for the propagation of the human race. But birth control and other frustrations of nature are even more against the natural law, because they defy the means nature itself affords for this propagation.

Injustice (racial segregation, if it produces humiliation and injustice), disobedience to parents or lawful authority—in fact, everything covered by the Ten Commandments—are against the natural law.

Is the natural law known to all men? Every man capable of reason knows at least one precept of this law: Good is to be done, evil is to be avoided. This is as evident as that two and two make four.

A secondary class of precepts following from this is the broad principles of the Ten Commandments: Worship God, honor parents, do not kill the innocent, etc. These general precepts may be obscured for a time by miseducation, but they cannot long be unknown by anyone possessing the normal use of reason.

There is a third class of precepts of the natural law, which include the finer applications of the Commandments. These can often be known only after difficult study (unless, of course, one is brought up in an environment where these things are taken for granted). Even moral scientists do not claim to know all the remote applications of the natural law; the natural law will grow in our understanding until the end of time, although it will never change in itself.

The natural law was founded on the nature of God, and is as immutable as His own changeless mind. God was free to create or not to create, but once He creates He cannot change the essences of things; He cannot do things without a reason. He cannot free man from his duty to honor Him without denying Himself.

Thus God can no more change the natural law than He can make a circle square. He may change the matter of the law. He could, for instance, command Abraham to sacrifice Isaac, for He owned Isaac's life, and this sacrifice could obtain for Him a higher good, namely Abraham's utter obedience. But He could not have given Abraham permission simply to murder, for God must maintain order in His creation.

The same thing holds true for polygamy and divorce, permitted under the old law for a higher purpose. But theologians teach that God could not give permission for something like birth control, for this would be to nullify utterly His end. Similarly, God can dispense with some obligation that depends on the human will, but not on human nature. The worship of God is bound up with human nature; God cannot release man from that. It depends on the human will to keep a vow, and God can release from the obligation of that vow. This principle will be further explained in the discussion of exceptions to the indissolubility of marriage.

What Is the Divine Law?

All law comes from God, but the positive divine law is distinguished from the natural law in that it was made known by a special speech of God to man, first to Adam, then to the Patriarchs, then to Moses and the Prophets, and lastly, through Christ or the Holy Spirit, to the Apostles. Sometimes the divine law has the same subject as the natural law, e.g., the Ten Commandments and, with certain exceptions, the indissolubility of marriage. It is in the observance of the positive divine law that Christians should be distinguished from others.

The law of Christ includes the law of charity, whereby we love God and all men as sons of God and brothers of Christ. In addition to the law of charity and the Commandments, there are the sacramental laws, which command us to accept faith in Christ and be baptized, and receive other means of grace according to our state.

To these precepts are added the evangelical counsels, which Christ gave on the Mount and elsewhere, such as to forgive and forget injuries and to give all one's goods to the poor in order to follow a life of perfection. These counsels are not commanded to everybody, but are given to a chosen few, that they may more readily and perfectly reach their end. It is these counsels that are followed by the members of religious orders, as well as by many self-sacrificing people in the world.

Since the positive divine law is of God, no one, baptized or unbaptized, Catholic or not, may neglect it, once it is promulgated to him in the forum of his conscience. Thus no one is exempt from the obligation to receive Baptism and enter the Church, as soon as he knows that God has spoken, and spoken through the Church. No one, not even the unbaptized, may hinder the Church in her mission.

What Is Ecclesiastical Law?

One of the fundamentals of Catholicity, as I hinted before, is pluralism, the concept that one society is not all-competent for all the needs of man. It teaches that there are two sovereign societies in the world, one for man's spiritual needs, which is the Church, and the other for man's temporal needs, which is the state. Since man is body and soul, it follows that the spiritual penetrates the temporal and the temporal penetrates the spiritual. Hence both societies can make true laws, and the laws of neither need duplicate those of the other.

There is hardly any essential characteristic of a law of the state that cannot be found in a law of the Church. Both laws derive their authority from God, though ecclesiastical law does so more directly. Both bind in conscience; both provide penalties for their violation and machinery for their enforcement.

Ecclesiastical law takes various forms. Thus the term Apostolic Constitution designates all laws passed by the Pope, the supreme lawgiver in the Church. A *motu proprio* is a Pontifical law the Pope makes independently of others. Decrees are laws that the Pontiff makes in a general council or through the Roman Congregations; canons are the laws now collected in a code; statutes are the name for laws passed by Bishops. No Bishop may, however, enact a law against the general law of the Church. His writ runs only in his own diocese.

Who are subject to ecclesiastical law? Canon 87 of the Code of Canon Law states that "by Baptism a person becomes a subject of the Church of Christ, with all the rights and duties of a Christian, unless, as far as rights are concerned, there is some obstacle impeding the bond of communion with the Church, or a censure inflicted by the Church."

Hence pagans, Jews, and other unbaptized persons are only indirectly subject to purely ecclesiastical laws. But if they contract marriage with a Catholic, they must do so under the conditions laid down by the Church. With regard to Protestants and Oriental schismatics the same thing holds in practice, although they are theoretically regarded as subject to the laws of fasting and abstinence from meat and other laws relating to sanctification. They incur no guilt by violating these laws, since they are in good faith, but they should obey them once they recognize the Church's truth and authority. (Noldin, *Summa Theologiae Moralis*, N. 148)

Can There Be a Conflict Between Civil and Ecclesiastical Law?

Wherever the government does not recognize the Church's right to legislate in spiritual things and in matters of mixed spiritual and temporal character, there can be conflict. But this never need be, as was nobly stated by Leo XIII in his encyclical, *Immortale Dei*, November 1, 1885: "Between the two powers there must reign a well-ordered harmony. . . . To one power is committed directly and specifically the charge of what is helpful in worldly matters; whereas the other is to concern itself with the things that pertain to heaven and eternity.

"Everything, therefore, in human affairs that is in any way sacred, or has reference to the salvation of souls and the worship of God, whether by its nature or by its end, is subject to the jurisdiction and discipline of the Church. Whatever else is comprised in the civil and political order rightly comes under the authority of the State; for Christ commanded us to give to Caesar the things that are Caesar's, and to God the things that are God's."

A civil constitution can come into conflict with the laws of the Church only if it arrogates to itself an authority that does not belong to it, namely over the whole man, body and soul. This the United States Constitution does not pretend to do. As the Supreme Court said in the Oregon case of 1925: "The child is not the mere creature of the State." There are "other and higher ends" to which his parents may fit him. It is just these "higher ends" with which the law of the Church deals.

Let us take the question of a Catholic judge in a marriage case. Canon 1016 states that "the marriage of baptized persons is regulated not only by the divine law, but also by canon law, saving the competency of the civil power over the merely civil consequences of the marriage contract." This leaves no room for the dissolution of marriage by a civil judge.

On November 7, 1949, in an address to the Italian jurists, Pius XII restated a principle that has been much discussed in all moral theologies particularly since the secularizing laws of the Third French Republic in the 1880's. It contained nothing new in Catholic theology, but aroused the usual furor whenever the Pope pronounces on something touching marriage.

The Pontiff reminded the jurists that no judge could throw upon the civil law responsibility for an action that is against the natural law. This aroused great interest in the United States because of its application to divorce proceedings. The Pope, however, emphasized that there is a distinction between the approbation and the application of an unjust law. The judge may never show that he approves such a law, or recognizes in civil law a competency it does not possess; but, to avoid worse evils, he may simply declare that as far as the civil law is concerned, a marriage no longer exists. The "worse evil" would be, for example, the necessity for a good judge to resign.

The Catholic judge must have a good reason for passing

a decree of divorce; the grounds must be weighty; the judge must be convinced that the couple will not be reconciled. Since the civil law cannot touch the marriage bond, but can only dispose, as canon law declares, concerning some of the civil effects of marriage, this act can, for a good reason, be done in conscience by a civil judge.

The civil law, on its part, at least in the United States, does not claim all power over marriage. It could not do so under our Constitution, which forbids an establishment of religion or the prohibition of its free exercise. Therefore there is no essential conflict between American law, as constitutionally interpreted, and Church law.

The Church and the Civil Law

Church law and state law are not competitors, but each supplements the other. The Church makes its own the words of St. Paul: "Let everyone be subject to the higher authorities, for there exists no authority except from God, and those who exist have been appointed by God." (Rom. xiii, 1–3)

The Church has always held that even wicked or pagan lawgivers can enact laws that are binding in conscience. Sometimes she even makes the civil law her own, as in canon 1080, which declares that where the state makes adoption an impediment to marriage the Church also makes it an impediment.

In the exercise of her authority over Christian marriage the Church takes care to satisfy the conditions laid down by civil law. When the Church dissolves a marriage contracted by two unbaptized persons after one of the parties has been converted, and the other party will not live in peace with him (called the Pauline Privilege), this dissolution is granted only when a civil divorce is secured. If a couple are related within a degree forbidden by the state, the Church will not allow them to marry, even though an ecclesiastical dispensation has been secured, until the matter is cleared with the civil law. (Connell, *Relationship Between Church and State*, p. 17)

Sometimes the same offense is punished in both canon and civil laws. A prime example is abortion, which according to canon 1350 incurs excommunication for all concerned. Often the concerns of both state and Church are the same, though in different ways. The state, like religious orders and private citizens, can establish hospitals and orphanages where necessary, and provide for education. It can and should protect good morals, without which no nation can long endure.

In matters merely temporal the state can enact laws independently of the Church, but not independently of God. It can force parents to support their children, and children to support their parents; it can determine what is necessary for contracts and inheritances, and fill out the natural law in any number of other ways, provided only it leaves the natural law itself intact.

In mixed matters, which have both a spiritual and a temporal end, the state can determine certain conditions to secure its interests. Thus it can prescribe the teaching of American history and the civil rights and duties of husband and wife and children. But it cannot monopolize education, or loose the bond of a valid marriage.

As regards unjust laws, these are ordinarily lacking in binding force, save indirectly, to avoid worse evils. A law that commands something against the natural law, such as the sterilization of an innocent man, could not be obeyed, since it is no proper law. If a law commands what is not by its nature unjust, but is opposed to the rights of the Church, there can be an obligation to obey externally, for the sake of civil peace. An example is the conscription law of France, which drafts priests into the army. This category of laws is inexhaustible.

The right of rebellion against unjust laws or tyrannical governments has always been recognized by Catholic moralists. Its exercise, however, is subject to certain conditions, which rarely occur in practice. The conditions are the same as those that apply to the waging of a just war; namely, that there be no peaceable way to remedy an unbearable evil and that the end sought is commensurate with the evils that inevitably follow rebellion.

Chapter 12

Conscience and Sin

CONSCIENCE usually follows law as a subject of inquiry by Catholic theologians, and for a good reason: conscience presupposes a law outside itself. It is in fact a practical judgment of reason on the moral rightness or wrongness of an action, an act of the intellect judging that here and now this must be avoided or that must be done.

Since conscience is a moral judgment, it is subject to the limitations of the reason when it judges; consequently, it can be true or erroneous, certain or uncertain, lax or narrow. Catholic theology rarely or never handles any term without distinguishing and subdistinguishing it; its genius is hostile to mystification.

In Catholic theology, conscience is not regarded as an independent emotional faculty, for which no one owes an accounting. When moral theology speaks of the rights of conscience it has in mind the rights of the Creator, who makes His law known through conscience as its herald. Conscience has rights because it has duties. These rights are not the rights of self-will.

A *certain* conscience must always be obeyed when it commands or forbids, since conscience is the only way God's law is made known to the individual. Thus a Protestant, certain of the truth of his religion, would commit sin by becoming a Catholic. The Fourth Council of the Lateran (1215) declared: "He who acts against his conscience loses his soul."

Though it is wrong for me to act against a certain conscience, even though it be actually mistaken, once I begin to suspect the truth I am bound to inquire further. Otherwise my conscience ceases to be certain and a messenger of God.

What Catholicity respects in conscience—and no other religion respects conscience so highly—is not the individual's understanding, which may be egregiously wrong, but God. God cannot impose error on anyone, but He is not bound to remove all the human conditions that make for error. And in all consciences, false or true, this thing remains true: God imposes an obligation. That is why Hermann Busenbaum, the seventeenth-century Jesuit theologian accused of teaching that "the end justifies the means," could write:

"When men who have been brought up in heresy are persuaded from boyhood that we Catholics impugn and attack the word of God, that we are idolaters, pestilent deceivers, and therefore to be shunned as pests, they cannot, while this persuasion lasts, listen to us with a safe conscience." (*Medulla Theologiae Moralis*, I, p. 54)

Sincerity does not make an error truth, but it does excuse one from sin in holding to the error that he thinks to be truth. That is why the Catholic Church has never sanctioned the punishment of anyone for sincerely believing an error. Theologians hold that if a Catholic erroneously believed a precept of the Pope, a Bishop, or a priest to be morally wrong, he is not bound to obey these superiors, and that he would commit a sin if he did.

But the very fact that conscience is the application by the individual intellect of a principle of the objective moral law to a particular action also explains why both state and Church may protect the true consciences of their people from the erroneous (even if sincere) consciences of some. Conscience and the moral law are not the same thing, as even the most liberal civil law must recognize. Only recently a Utah court took away the children of parents who believed in and taught their offspring polygamy. No one has the right to impose his own erring conscience on the right consciences of others, to the hurt of the common good.

Famous in the history of American law is the case of People vs. Ruggles, in which Chancellor James Kent of the New York Court of Chancery, deciding against a defendant in a blasphemy case, declared that "liberty of conscience . . . shall not be so construed as to excuse acts of licentiousness, or justify practices inconsistent with the peace and safety of the State."

The Catholic Church follows this dictum in sanctioning the action of civil authorities in enforcing the public law made to protect the faith of the people and the public peace against open attacks made upon both by heretics and unbelievers. In Colombia, for example, Catholics everywhere want freedom of conscience to prevail. But it is no secret that they are with the Colombian law and against certain fanatical sectarians, when these zealots attack the Colombian Hierarchy, misrepresent the religion of the majority of Colombians, and insult the Virgin Mary, who is far more sacred to Colombians than Washington or Lincoln is to us. This is not the repression of conscience. It is the maintenance of the public peace.

Catholics, it must be remembered, put themselves under the same restrictions of good taste and prudence as they expect in others. The early Church refused the honors of martyrdom to any Christian put to death for outraging or overturning an idol. In more recent times the Holy See forbade Christians, whether clergy or laity, to provoke Mohammedans to controversy and refused the title of martyr to those who brought death on themselves by speaking against Mohammed. (*Dictionnaire apologétique,* IV, col. 11)

Sin and Moral Theology

After the moral law and conscience comes sin, which transgresses the one and defies the other. Cardinal Newman expressed the Catholic attitude toward sin in this classical statement from his *Anglican Difficulties:*

"The Church holds that it were better for sun and moon to drop from heaven, for the earth to fail, and for all the many millions who are upon it to die of starvation in extremest agony, so far as temporal affliction goes, than that one soul, I will not say should be lost, but should commit one single venial sin, should tell one wilful untruth, though it harmed no one, or steal one poor farthing without excuse." (p. 190)

Sin is the free transgression of the order established by God. Three things determine every sin: (a) an action that is against the law of God, and therefore a bad action; (b) the advertence of the mind to the badness of the action; (c) the consent of the will. If one of these three conditions is entirely absent there is no sin; the diminution of any one of them greatly reduces its gravity.

One of the great marks of the reasonableness of Catholicity is its distinction between mortal and venial sins, a distinction not clearly drawn in any other religion. A mortal sin occurs when one transgresses the law of God in a grave matter, with full notice of what is done and complete consent. It is called *mortal* because it brings spiritual death. A venial sin is a transgression in a light matter, or, if in a grave matter, with incomplete notice of the evil of the act or incomplete consent thereto. A sin grave in itself becomes venial for the individual if he thinks it venial at the time, and conversely a venial sin becomes mortal for the individual if he thinks when he does it that it is a mortal sin. If I think that perjury is a venial sin, and commit perjury, then it would be venial for me, though it is mortal in itself. In fact, if I think that I am morally bound to lie in order to save someone I would be sinning if I did not tell what is objectively a lie.

Some sins are objectively grave whenever we commit them. Such are all sins of impurity. Others are ordinarily always venial, unless aggravated by some circumstance. Such are common lies. Others may be venial or mortal according to the matter involved. For instance, theft is defined as the taking of property against the reasonable will of the owner. Within limits, the more one has the less unwilling one is to have a small amount stolen. But beyond $75 theft from anyone, no matter how rich, would be a mortal sin, since it would undermine the common good.

In general, all sins that result in grave injustice to God (such as blasphemy); grave injury to a neighbor; grave injury to the human race, the Church, or the state; or grave injury to one's own welfare are mortal sins.

Take the act of impurity, for example. The reason why all such deliberate sins are mortal is that they strike at the welfare of the entire human race. If sex pleasure, even in thought or desire, could be sought outside marriage few would undertake marriage's burdens, and the race would become extinct. A sin of impurity is, in short, the preference of an individual pleasure to the good of the human race, and thus is a grave disorder. All sin is disorder in some way.

Chapter 13

Between Faith and Charity

ALL RELIGIONS are commonly called "faiths," and so they are in a wide human sense. But Judaism and Catholicity are the only religions characterized by faith in a divine revelation. Mohammedanism, Protestantism, and to some extent even Buddhism, owe their faith in revelation either to derivations from Catholicity or (as in the case of Mohammedanism and Buddhism) to imitations of it. The mythologies of the primitives and the East Indians can hardly be called faiths in our sense.

Catholicity is called by Belloc "the Faith," as by its proper name. No other name, drawn from the theological virtues, so well befits it, unless we use the term Ignatius of Antioch employed, "the Charity."

Theologians teach that it is absolutely necessary for anyone who would save his soul to believe at least two truths: that God exists and that He rewards or punishes in the future life according to one's deeds in this. The weight of opinion is that belief in the Trinity and the Incarnation is not required for the salvation of one who cannot be expected to know them, for example, a pagan to whom the Faith has been insufficiently preached. This is a fair specimen of a seemingly contradictory thing, to wit, an opinion that is "more probable" but "less safe," of which there are many instances in moral theology. That is, it is more probable in theory but not safe, because uncertain, to apply in practice; thus whenever possible a candidate for Baptism must be instructed in the doctrines of the Trinity and the Incarnation.

The Church requires all Catholics to know substantially the Apostles' Creed, the Ten Commandments, the six commandments of the Church, the essential duties of life according to one's state (as marriage, the duties of employer and employee, of a citizen, etc.), the Lord's Prayer, and the fundamentals of the sacraments that one is to receive. It is not strictly necessary, but required under a light obligation, to know the exact words of the Creed, Lord's Prayer, and Commandments, and also the sign of the cross and the Hail Mary. All Catholics must accept every definition of faith when proposed by the Church.

Since faith is the beginning and mainspring of Christian life, it is easy to understand why the Church surrounds it with such safeguards—why she insists on the establishment, whenever possible, of Catholic schools, to which the faithful are obliged to send their children. "Catholic children are to be educated in schools where not only nothing contrary to Catholic faith and morals is taught, but rather in schools where religious and moral training occupy the first place." (can. 1372)

Since in Catholic teaching the sins against faith are, after the hatred of God, the gravest that can be committed, it is never permitted to attend a school where it is certain that there will be a danger to Catholic faith that cannot be avoided. An instruction of the Holy Office to the Bishops of the United States, dated November 24, 1875, declared that the danger of perversion (loss of faith) must be "absolutely avoided, at the price of any temporal loss whatever, be it even that of life."

Does Catholicity Admit the Sincerity of Non-Catholics Who Know the Church?

The Vatican Council declared that those who received the faith under the ecclesiastical teaching office can never have any good reason for changing or doubting it. (D. 1794)

A poorly instructed person, brought up in hostile surroundings, might leave the Church in good faith, but not one who has learned the fundamentals prescribed by the Church.

Most non-Catholics do not know the Church; if they did, many of them would become Catholics. But it is freely admitted that even those acquainted with her claims may, for a time at least, continue in good faith in their own beliefs. Suarez, the great sixteenth-century Spanish theologian, and his fellow theologians of the University of Salamanca in Spain, writing in an age and a country where the Catholic faith reigned undisputed, declared that even in such an environment there could be sincere heretics or unbelievers, who never experience any doubt about the truth of their religion. (*Dictionnaire de la théologie catholique;* art "Eglise," col. 2167)

The great English Cardinal, William Manning, himself a former Anglican minister, observed that "it is only after a long time, and much prayer and study, that the most gifted minds, born in heresy, come to understand that their Church is not the true one. When you propose to anyone, even if very intelligent, a riddle of which you have the solution, you are surprised to see your listener hesitate, grope about, and not find a solution that to you appears childishly simple. Give him the explanation he is looking for, and he will himself be surprised at not discovering it at once. So it is with the best instructed and sincerest heretic: He may study and pray a long time without being enlightened; and then, only at a certain moment, marked by grace, does he find the truth, and is surprised at not finding it sooner." (Tanquerey, *Synopsis theologiae Moralis,* II, p. 474, note) But the Church insists that the evidences for the Catholic religion are in themselves fully sufficient to convince anyone.

Why Do Catholics Not Associate with Non-Catholics in Religious Functions?

It is only in public functions that this religious association is forbidden. Non-Catholics may not serve as godparents at a Catholic Baptism, may not serve Mass, or take part in processions. Catholics may for good reason act as ushers at a non-Catholic wedding, but not as witnesses; Catholics who contract marriage before a non-Catholic clergyman are excommunicated. A Catholic may attend a funeral or wedding of a friend, but not take part in religious acts.

These restrictions are not because of arrogance, to which the Church is a stranger. The basic reason is the fact that the only religious body authorized by Christ to conduct divine services is the Catholic Church. Catholics by their presence seem to lend their sanction to a form of worship, which, though it may be good in itself and of great help to those who participate in it, is not divinely authorized worship. (Connell, *Outlines of Moral Theology,* p. 76)

A second reason is that, were participation in non-Catholic services allowed, Catholics would be absorbed in another religious community that is not of God. The liberal Protestant Church historian, Kenneth Latourette, explains this danger in the case of the Chinese (Confucian) Rites, which were a center of controversy in the Church two centuries ago. Since 1938 these rites have been officially recognized as having only a civil character, and therefore allowable to Chinese Christians:

"It must be said for the Papal decrees [against Catholic Chinese participation in the rites] that they helped to keep the Church from losing its distinctive message and probably its vitality. Had the Church made its peace with some of the more important existing religious practices of China, deterioration would almost certainly have followed." (*History of Christian Missions in China,* p. 155)

This historian, let me add, was much fairer to the eighteenth-century Popes than many Catholic historians, who saw (far too easily) in the prohibition of participation in the rites the loss of China to the Church.

There is a vast area, involving religion and morals, in which Catholics are encouraged to co-operate with non-Catholics. Such is the fight against atheistic Communism, the campaign for decency in movies and the press, the struggle against racial discrimination and for social justice, the war against alcoholism. Alcoholics Anonymous, founded by a non-Catholic, and with a strong religious coloring, has received the enthusiastic co-operation of many priests. On the other hand, the Buchmanite, or Moral Rearmament Movement, has been discountenanced by some European Bishops as tending to religious indifferentism.

Here is the principle governing Catholic co-operation in movements of a non-Catholic nature. Wherever the movement is not sectarian, or does not form a religion by itself; wherever it does not tend to foster the idea that one religion is as good as another; wherever it aims for a purely civic end, though it be animated by a religious spirit, then Catholics as citizens may and should take part. In fact, the shoe is most often on the other foot. Many sectarian leaders, though by no means all, will refuse to join in a Catholic campaign for decency in the films, or will even refuse to support Catholic protests against religious persecution behind the Iron Curtain, simply because of a fear that Catholicity might benefit. Catholicity, I repeat, is jealous, not envious. Innumerable are the Papal pronouncements calling on all men of good will to introduce into the world a reign of moral law. If some non-Catholic religious organization, like the Quakers, is eminent for philanthropy, Catholic publications gladly record it. In the *Register* of January 2, 1955, there appeared a generous article recording the fact that many non-Catholics give far more to religion than most Catholics. (p. 2, col. 3)

Why Does the Church Prohibit Books Against the Faith?

The Church has always taken a realistic view of the human mind. She knows it bears a close analogy to the body. It is not necessary to drink poison in order to prove you have a good stomach. The Church does not forbid books because she fears for the truth of what she teaches, but because she fears human frailty.

As a matter of fact, the Catholic parochial school child—to say nothing of the Catholic college student—ordinarily knows far more of the views of the adversaries of his faith than the adversaries generally know about Catholic doctrine. In high-school and even grade-school religion classes, the teacher will pose as an unbeliever, who rebuts answer after answer until the one that would satisfy a competent defender of the faith comes forth.

As long as there is an adequate reply in the same book to the attacks of opponents of Catholic doctrine, both Catholic and opponent may write in that book, and it is freely circulated among the faithful. The Arnold Lunn debate books, such as *Is the Catholic Church Anti-Social?*, in which that noted apologist gave a space equal to what he occupied to a prominent and skilled controversialist attacking the Church, have enjoyed popularity among Catholics. When the book *Is the Catholic Church Anti-Social?* was to be published in 1947, G. G. Coulton, the historian who has so often criticized the Church, tried in vain to find a Protestant publisher, but the book was published by Burns, Oates, English publishers to the Holy See. (*Op. cit.,* p. 152)

Any book that could induce a danger to faith or morals is prohibited under canon 1399 of the Code of Canon Law. These include all versions of Sacred Scripture unless published with ecclesiastical approval and provided with suitable notes. Serious students of the Bible may use additions of Scripture edited by non-Catholics as long as the books are faithful and complete copies of the original and do not attack Catholic dogmas.

Books *defending* (not merely explaining) heresy are forbidden, as are, of course, all books purposely attacking religion or good morals or the Catholic Church in particular. Books of any non-Catholic professedly treating of religion are forbidden, unless it is certain they contain nothing against the faith. A religious novel like *The Robe,* written by a non-Catholic, is not forbidden, though it is not entirely unobjectionable from the Catholic standpoint.

The Index is by no means concerned solely with some non-Catholic authors. A frequent object of its prohibitions is non-approved devotions, though they may be written by perfectly sincere Catholics. In this class fall unauthorized liturgical books.

Books of magic and superstition, or those that defend dueling, suicide, divorce, or uphold condemned secret societies come under the Index; as does all pornography, even if it is written under the color of "sex instruction."

The written Index, consisting of some two thousand books compiled since 1600, is comparatively unimportant as a guide to the general reader. It is chiefly of concern to the scholar, as indicating what ideas are condemned by the Holy See. Every Catholic is expected to decide for himself, with guidance where necessary, what books are harmful according to the stipulations of canon 1399. It is freely admitted that some latitude is allowed for novels, which may harm one person and not another. Any book, however, that is generally harmful may not be read even by one who is not affected by it.

Anyone who has any business reading a serious book, even one grossly attacking the faith, such as Haeckel's *Riddle of the Universe,* need only write to the local Bishop's office, state the book desired, and the reasons for reading it. I personally have received speedy and favorable replies to all such applications.

What Is Catholic Teaching on the Salvation of Catholics and Non-Catholics?

Here we come to the theological virtue of hope, which is the infused habit inclining us with firm confidence to expect from God eternal life and the means of attaining it. It is Catholic teaching, confirmed by the Council of Trent (session vi, cap. 9 & 13), that: (1) no man should despair of the mercy of God, and (2) no man may, aside from a special revelation, be sure of his salvation. Therefore all must work out their salvation with fear, being careful to give alms, to pray, and to mortify themselves.

The Fourth Council of the Lateran (decree "Firmiter") declared: "If, after receiving Baptism, anyone falls into sin, he can always be restored by true penance." Alexander VIII condemned the proposition that "pagans, Jews, and heretics receive no influence at all from Jesus Christ." (Denz., 1295) Pius IX, in an encyclical dated August 10, 1863, laid it down that: "it is known to us and to you that those who suffer from invincible ignorance of our holy religion, but who conscientiously observe the natural law and its precepts, which are engraved on the hearts of all men, and are disposed to obey God and lead a virtuous and upright life, can, with the co-operative power of divine light and grace, attain eternal life." All this in no way dilutes the doctrine proclaiming the necessity of the Church, or some kind of relationship to it, for the salvation of every single human being. I shall discuss this in the chapter on The Church Sanctifying, under "Baptism of Desire." Here I shall add only that the idea of the salvation of those outside the Church, even the infidel, goes back to the beginning of Christian history, and we find a clear defense of it in the *Apology* (N. 46) of Justin Martyr (d. 165). "Never has theologian," remarked the great French infidel historian, Ernest Renan, "opened the gates of salvation so wide as has Justin."

Catholic doctrine is never sterile in social consequences. Let those who may be inclined to sneer at dogma reflect on this. It was the Catholic virtue of hope, along with that of love, that spoke in the eloquent bull of Paul IV (June 2, 1527), *Sublimis Deus,* in which he rebuked those Spaniards of Mexico who, to justify their rapacity, taught that the Indian was beyond hope of salvation:

"By these present letters we declare and determine . . . that the Indians and all the other nations that in the future shall come to the knowledge of Christians, even when those peoples lie outside the Faith, are nevertheless not deprived of liberty or ownership . . . nor must be reduced to slavery . . . and that the said Indians and other such nations are called to the said faith of Christ by means of the preaching of the word of God and the example of the good life."

Every nation that has taught absolute predestination— the doctrine that some are surely saved and others are surely damned—has had an unfortunate record when it has come into conflict with barbarian peoples. I am thinking of the Calvinist Boers of South Africa, whose three-century struggle with the Negroes is only now reaching a climax, and of the Puritans of New England. The fact that, by the mid-nineteenth century, there were 20,000,000 full-blooded Indians in the Spanish Americas, whereas there were perhaps 500,000 at that time in the United States, or that there are now 20,000,000 Filipinos, whereas there are now, at most,

20,000 pure-blooded Hawaiians (originally evangelized by New England Calvinist missionaries), seems to argue that the theological doctrine of hope has incalculable consequences on this earth alone.

Because of the theological virtue of hope, Catholics may never teach the existence of accursed races. It was first put forward in 1677 by a Calvinist doctor (Jan Hannemann), and was later used in our South to justify slavery. (*Osservatore Romano,* col. "Leggende e Storia," Feb. 18, 1951)

How Charity Rules the Church

"Ignatius . . . to the Church beloved and illumined by His will, which wills all that is according to the love of Jesus Christ Our God, which also presides in the place of the country of the Romans, worthy of God, worthy of glory, worthy to be called blessed, worthy of praise, worthy to be desired, worthily chaste, presiding over the universal assembly of the Love." Thus did Ignatius of Antioch address the Church of Rome in the year 107. And in placing *love* at the summit of his honorifics he indicated the most distinctive title the Catholic religion can have.

As the highest of the theological virtues, charity is defined as that infused habit, which inclines us to love God above all things for His sake, and everything that God loves for the sake of Him.

We cannot rightly love God unless we love His works, especially those that most reflect His goodness—that work, in short, which reflects His image, man. Voltaire spoke better than he knew when he said, in a letter to d'Alembert, December 6, 1757: "I have never claimed to enlighten old jades and servant girls; that is the Prerogative of the Apostles."

The Church of the Apostles goes to great trouble to enlighten old jades, for she knows they have a soul that Christ would have died to save, could He have saved none but old jades. This precept to love our neighbors as God loves them, and not as we like them, explains, with God's help, the enormous fecundity of the Church in charitable works among all nations—her missions over all the world; her leprosariums, staffed by sisters for want of others who will do this repulsive work; her constant fight against race prejudice and for the poor and oppressed. The Pope, cruelly as he has been anguished by Communist persecution, has sent messages of love to the peoples of China, Russia, and Romania. The Church can never hate anyone.

Charity gives rise to a whole hierarchy of obligations. Since our first responsibility is to our own souls, we must love first our spiritual welfare. We can never hurt our soul to help another. Love of self is opposed to egotism, which loves, not self truly, but rather comfort, to the prejudice of God and neighbor and ourselves.

If someone is in extreme spiritual need, so that he will surely die and be lost unless I help him, and I am reasonably sure I am in the state of God's friendship, I must give even my life to help him. The only case in which this might be verified would be that of an imperiled unbaptized baby.

If our neighbor is in extreme temporal necessity, that is, in imminent danger of death, one must save him at the risk of one's own life, if he be of vital importance to the community. In other cases, one must at least go to great temporal inconvenience to help him.

And so this obligation of love descends through the degrees of binding force, the spiritual coming before the bodily welfare but both demanding succor. A pastor or physician may be obliged to give his life in the service of those suffering from plague. A married man should prefer, in case of grave necessity, his wife to his children and both to his parents; but in case of extreme necessity, when it is a question of saving the life of one and letting another go, parents must be preferred to wife and children, for parents are the cause of our existence.

If a certain poor man is ill, and there is no other doctor to help him, that doctor has a grave duty to help him gratis. In ordinary need, charity obliges us to help the poor in general from our superfluous possessions—say 5 to 7 per cent, as far as a strict obligation is concerned. (Connell, *Outlines of Moral Theology*, p. 91)

In the matter of charity Catholic theology reasons according to the rule of the Master: it avoids both senseless sacrifice and egotism.

But charity in the Catholic concept extends to far wider fields than almsgiving or the saving of bodily life. Curiously, this commandment of love must be exercised in ways that often arouse intense opposition to the Church.

One of the gravest duties of charity is the obligation not to give scandal. *Scandal* is one of those words which, since they are used by Catholicity in the precise sense, often are not understood by non-Catholics, who may get a picture of an old lady in ringlets holding up two outspread hands in shocked surprise. Scandal in Catholic usage means primarily what the name implies—a stumbling-block (*scandalum*), over which the neighbor trips and falls into spiritual ruin. It may be rendered roughly as "bad example."

Scandal is anything said or done that is either evil or has the appearance of evil and may cause another to fall into sin. Parents who speak disrespectfully of teachers before their children; landlords who exclude families with more than two children, and thereby offer temptation to birth control; girls who take part in bathing beauty contests offer scandal. Scandal may be committed in every walk of life.

More directly against the good of the neighbor's soul is co-operation in evil. This co-operation is only material if the act itself is good, but helps another to commit evil. In such cases, the more remote the co-operation the more easily will it be permitted, provided some proportionate reason is present. The closer the co-operation the greater is the reason demanded, until finally no reason will justify it.

Thus no reason of profit will justify a pharmacist in selling articles that can be used only for birth control, and that regardless of whether his customers are Catholic or not, in good faith or not. But the pharmacist's clerk, who gives merely material co-operation in making the sale, can be excused, if otherwise he will find it hard to get another job.

Catholic hospitals may not allow the physicians on their staff to perform sterilizations or abortions or any other unlawful operation, regardless of whether the surgeons are Catholic or not. No nurse may give either formal or immediate co-operation in an intrinsically immoral act. An example would be instruction in the use of contraceptives under order of her superior. Only for a grave reason may she assist the surgeon at an immoral operation by handing him the instruments he may require. The principle is that we are all under obligation as far as possible to keep our neighbor from committing sin, even though he be sincere. An African witch doctor who commands his "patient" to take a cupful of blood from the veins of a living man may be sincere; certainly his "patient" may be. He is not justified on that account, even though the popular sense in his region would support him.

Those who rail against the Church for "intolerance" in her demands that the natural law be observed should, in the Catholic view, consider whether the roles may not be reversed. Is not the secularist, who admits that he has no fixed moral standards, trying to force his own concepts on the Catholic, rather than the reverse?

One who acts according to what he claims is the natural law is in possession over one who says he does not know what the natural law rules. It is up to the latter to prove that the one who claims a knowledge of the natural law has misunderstood it. At any rate, one who believes in a universal, immutable natural law cannot be blamed for acting consistently with that belief.

Chapter 14

The Church and the Commandments

THE TEN COMMANDMENTS contain implicitly all that is required to reach our heavenly goal. The commandments of the Church, which are six in number, can be included under the Fourth Commandment, which demands obedience to lawful superiors, or under the First and Second Commandments, which bid us give worship to God. Hence it is that the moral theologians usually divide their treatise on precepts according to the Decalogue.

The First Commandment brings up the question of worship, which is a debt of justice due to God. All Catholics understand that the various grades of reverence paid to relics, images, crucifixes, the saints, and the Blessed Virgin are ultimately referred to God. As I indicated in the previous chapter, you never find any confusion on this point, even among ill-instructed Catholics.

No religion places so much reliance on prayer as does the Catholic. Relying on the promises of Christ: "Whatever you shall ask the Father in My name, He shall give you . . ." (John xvi, 23–24), the Church teaches that every prayer is heard if we pray with humility, confidence, and perseverance. All answers to prayer have reference to our eternal salvation, but material benefits can be prayed for, since they may redound to our eternal good.

No Catholic who is a good Catholic lets a night or a morning pass without saying his prayers; no good Catholic home omits grace at meals. Common prayers are the Lord's Prayer and the Hail Mary, based on the words the angel Gabriel addressed to the Virgin. These form the principal prayers of the rosary, a string of beads consisting of five (or, sometimes, six) Our Fathers and fifty Hail Marys. The public prayer of the Church is found chiefly in the Mass and the Divine office, which priests and nuns and brothers who have taken solemn vows must read every day. The Office consists largely of excerpts from the Psalms and the Gospels, together with sections from the lives of the saints, and varies from day to day. It usually takes an hour to read, and the reading often offers a severe exercise in discipline to the busy priest. But I have had one of them tell me he would not forgo it even if it were not imposed on him. The Breviary, or Office, contains some of the most beautiful outpourings of the religious spirit.

All superstitious observances, all unauthorized cults come under the ban of the First Commandment. The Church will hear nothing of anything savoring of spiritualism, divination, and magic; she is slow to accept reported apparitions of the Blessed Virgin. When in 1950 a great stir was created in a certain United States diocese by an alleged visionary, the edition of the *Register* for that diocese was told by the Bishop to say absolutely nothing about it, in order to quiet the interest aroused. There are few things about which Bishops are less indulgent than a dubious apparition. The assertion that the Church encourages stories of private revelations is one of the most baseless of the calumnies about her.

The hearing of Mass is a grave obligation in the Church, and the culpable omission of it on Sunday or a holy day constitutes a mortal sin. The regular hearing of Mass, together with the reception of the sacraments at least once a year, is one of the marks that determine a practical Catholic. Catholics of fervor will go to Mass daily if they have opportunity.

Regarding the Sabbath rest, theology takes its usual moderate course. Today there is an increasing tendency among theologians to consider not so much the nature of the work done on a holy day, but whether it so enslaves the mind as to create an obstacle to the cultivation of man's spiritual life. Light manual labor, whatever its nature, as long as it is done for recreation or to avoid idleness, does not create this obstacle. But mere greed, whether of employer or employee, must not be the motive for working on Sunday. The liberal pursuits, such as writing or teaching (even for pay), are not deemed to violate the Sunday rest. No wholesome recreation is disallowed as long as it does not interfere with religious duties.

The Fourth Commandment (Honor Thy Father and Mother) comprises a long range of duties included under the name of piety. The term is well chosen. Our relations with our parents and our country recall the creative action of the Omnipotent. We owe "piety" to parents and country because they will always remain, in relation to God, a secondary cause of our existence, after its first great Principle. Hence moral science has borrowed a word from religion to express the duties owed to family and nation.

Piety requires that children show their parents obedience, reverence, and love. The obligation of children to support their parents in time of need never ceases throughout life. A child would not be allowed to enter a religious order if his or her parents were in grave necessity. The Church decrees that a pastor shall not assist at the marriage of minors when the parents are reasonably unwilling (can. 1034). Even older children, as long as they remain under the parental roof, are bound to obey their parents in all reasonable regulations.

The obligation of piety flows back from parents to children. As soon as it is evident that a child has been conceived there is a grave obligation not to do anything to injure it. Parents must afford their children food, clothing, shelter, and education up to the time in which they can fend for themselves. They must use at least ordinary diligence to lay away an inheritance for them.

Parents must have their children baptized as soon as possible, so that they may be citizens of the Church and candidates for heaven. From their tenderest years they must teach them the mysteries of the faith and imbue them with a love of Christ the Mediator and His Mother; early they must accustom them to saying their prayers and hearing Mass. Where possible they must send them to Catholic schools, and wherever possible they are bound to erect these schools, which they do at great sacrifice. In 1954 a Department of Commerce report found that $560,000,000 was spent for private-school building, and most of this came from Catholic hands.

Children, even under age, are not bound to obey their parents in their choice of vocation.

Catholic practice and teaching have always upheld reasonable discipline, even to the use of the rod. The *Roman Catechism,* one of the most authoritative manuals of religious instruction, being edited by the later Papal Secretary of State, Cardinal Gasparri, states: "If any fault has been committed, since chastisement and rebuke are necessary against indiscipline, children must not, as often happens, be spoiled by the overindulgence of their parents."

The Catholic ideal of education is the man, whole and entire, soul united to body, with all his faculties, natural and supernatural, as right, reason, and revelation show him to be—man, therefore, fallen from his original state, but redeemed by Christ. Disorderly inclinations must be corrected, good tendencies encouraged. (Pius XI, *Christian Education of Youth*) Children must learn gradually to think, will, and act for themselves independently of human respect, but never independently of God.

As we saw in philosophy, the ideal of the Catholic family is a hierarchy, with the father in the most important place and the mother next, and all members owing one another mutual duties. The wife has the right to manage family matters independently of her husband; the husband sins if he refuses to provide his wife with proper support according to her state. Both husband and wife must bear with each other's frailties.

As in the natural society of marriage the sexes are equal by nature but have different duties, so the natural constitution of man and woman carries over into wider life. The Church, recognizing that woman has a particular destiny, determined on the one hand by her physical and spiritual constitution, and on the other by the role she is to fulfill in the family, insists that in studies, work, sports, and the manifold distractions of life her modesty must be protected and her strength and aptitudes taken into account. Catholics have always opposed legislation that would treat man and woman as if they were exactly the same, for this would be the greatest inequality. The admission of woman to offices and professions for which she is either equally well suited as man, or more so, and which are not incompatible with her sex, meets no obstacle in the Church. What greater executives are there than the superioresses of large religious orders or congregations? But exaggerated feminism goes against the Catholic grain.

What Is Catholic Teaching on Political Duties?

Public authority is bound to recognize, regulate, and promote the inalienable rights of individuals and families. Its powers are great, but limited. "Public authority," wrote Pius XII in his encyclical, *Summi Pontificatus,* "may exact blood and treasure, but never the soul that has been redeemed by God."

The state is bound to avert temporal evils and dangers, administer justice without favoritism, entrust offices to fit and worthy men, and to keep its taxes from absorbing private wealth.

Citizens must pay taxes, obey the laws, and co-operate for the common good. Democratic governments impose on the people a special duty to interest themselves in politics, which may be binding under pain of grave sin. The Church has not hesitated to make this clear by special decree in those European countries threatened by Communism.

Thus in August, 1945, the Consistorial Congregation invited the Bishops of Italy to inform their faithful of the following norms of voting taken from moral theology: "In consideration of the dangers to which religion and the public good are exposed . . . all those who have the right to vote, of whatever condition, sex, or age without exception, are in conscience strictly bound to use that right. Catholics can give their vote only to those candidates who they are certain will respect and defend the observance of the divine law and the rights of religion and the Church in public and private life."

Not a man in the world but benefited by that exercise of ecclesiastical authority.

"In a democratic state the citizen must, more than other citizens, be enlightened, honest, and solicitous for the common good. The candidate does not, by the mere fact of his candidature, renounce the right of protection for his private life. At election time the rights of truth, justice, and charity must be respected." (Tanquerey, *Synopsis Theologiae Moralis*, III, N. 984)

The Commandment Not to Kill

All Catholic doctrine is simple in principle, though its application grows more difficult the more involved becomes the case. Anyone, however, can understand that if man is put here for a purpose then his body is not his own. He may not directly injure either himself or another, any more than he could do what he wills with another's property.

This principle explains the following prohibitions: direct suicide; indirect suicide (i.e., by abuse of one's body); self-mutilation; sterilization. Direct suicide is never allowed for whatever good; the other evils are allowed only for a proportionately grave reason. Note again how the end as a determinant of the moral act keeps cropping up in moral theology. We live in the world, and it is impossible for us to avoid all actions that may contribute to the neighbor's sin or to our own hurt. The only absolute rule we can lay down is that an intrinsically evil act, such as direct suicide, may never be done, and that other acts, not intrinsically evil but leading to evil, may be done only for proportionate reason.

Catholicity teaches the equality of all human nature far more consistently and thoroughly than any other religion or thought system. It never allows one innocent life to be taken for the benefit of another. That is why abortion, strictly so called, is never permitted. What the theologians call "indirect" abortion is really not abortion but the removal of a diseased condition. That a child perishes in such an operation happens only accidentally; is permitted, not willed. Moral theology always goes back to its principles, which seem so dry and abstract at first—the human act, the voluntary act, the directly and indirectly voluntary act. Everything Catholic fits into a system; nothing exists in isolation.

What is the Catholic teaching on capital punishment? Many Catholic countries have abolished the system altogether. Portugal, with no sentence heavier than twenty-eight years' imprisonment, has one of the mildest criminal codes in the world. Nevertheless, Catholic moralists are generally favorable to the death penalty; none could, in fact, condemn it, since it is based on the injunction of St. Paul to "fear those who carry the sword" (Rom. xiii, 4) and "Whoever shall shed man's blood, his blood shall be shed." (Gen. ix, 6)

This justification is also drawn from the theological reason that a man who has committed a heinous crime has withdrawn himself from the inviolability that protects a man of reason, and therefore can be punished as if he had no reason—as a beast. Even a condemned criminal has, of course, inalienable rights, and must be allowed time to prepare for his end. An unjust aggressor may be killed to protect life or goods of great value, but if he can be stopped by action less than what produces death this should be done.

Catholicity and War

The conditions that justify war are basically no different than those that justify the killing of a private assailant. If killing to save the life that is attacked by a robber is justified, then so also can be the killing of a public enemy. As long as no universal and obligatory rule of law exists in the world, which will protect nations from assault, then war under certain conditions must remain legitimate.

Moralists, even until recent years, held that it is legitimate to undertake offensive (not aggressive) war, to repair serious rights violated by a nation that would not give satisfaction. An offensive war can certainly in itself be just, if waged for a proportionate reason, just as police may move against a recalcitrant citizen. But the destructiveness of modern war, particularly if world-wide, has made it impossible to see how the proportionate reason could now exist. In the unreserved condemnation of every modern offensive war most Catholic moralists who have expressed themselves are agreed. (*Herders Sozial-Katechismus*, II, N. 132) This, of course, does not mean that a nation unjustly attacked could not take the offensive to defend itself.

Pius XII, in his Christmas Eve message of 1944, declared: "A duty lies on everyone—a duty that brooks no delay, no evasion, no hesitation, no postponement—to banish aggressive war as a solution of international tensions."

But the obligation of defense in case of unjustified attack was likewise enforced by the Pontiff in his 1948 peace message: "A people that is threatened by unjust attack, or is already its victim, may not, if it wishes to act in a Christian manner, remain in passive indifference; even more does the solidarity of the family of nations forbid the others to stand aloof in unfeeling neutrality. . . . This is so true that neither the exclusive consideration of the sufferings and evils caused by war, nor the close calculation of its loss and gain, can finally determine whether it is morally permitted or obligatory under certain concrete conditions [provided there is a well-founded probability of success] to repel the aggressor with force. . . . There are among these goods of the Creator many of such importance for human coexistence that their defense against unjust aggression is without doubt perfectly justified."

War is therefore justified, but only as a last resort to save goods more precious than life.

What Does Catholic Morality Say About the Use of Atomic or Hydrogen Bombs?

The various pronouncements of Pius XII are summed up in the words of *Herders Sozial-Katechismus*, II, N. 131: "There exists at most one reason for the use of modern weapons, the extreme need of protection in a just defensive war. Practically, this reason will obtain only when . . . it is certain that no other means is available to save the state's existence from the attacks of an aggressor. Thus neither mere reprisal nor the prospect of shortening the war suffices. It is never permitted to use weapons against a population that takes part in the war only remotely, even in the hope of breaking down their will to fight."

The Church and Sex Morality

The principle governing sexual relations in the Catholic conception is as simple as that respecting the taking of life. It can be stated in one sentence. *Man may not use the generative faculty beyond its spiritual content.* The sexual function and the enjoyment thereof are intended by nature's God for the propagation of the race in stable wedlock. Accordingly, any use of such function outside this condition—even any thought or desire leading to it—is mortally sinful.

As I explained before, the reason why every sin of lust is grave is that it represents an attack on the entire human race. If the sex instinct could be satisfied in any other way than in marriage the world would soon become extinct. Of course, degrees of gravity in this sin vary greatly. Internal sins (thoughts, desires) are not so grave as external, consummated sins, and consummated sins are grave in proportion to their opposition to nature.

Although the sin of impurity is not reckoned among the graver mortal sins—spiritual sins, such as those against faith are much more serious as a class—a peculiar foulness attaches to lust, if committed by a Christian, that is not found in other sins. For the body of a Christian, which has been washed with the blood of Christ through Baptism and made a temple of God by the indwelling of the Holy Spirit, is profaned and accursed by a sin of the flesh.

The seriousness with which the Church regards the sacredness of sex explains the importance she attaches to modesty, which is the virtue protecting chastity. Immodest dress in woman, tantalizing prints and pictures—everything that ordinarily starts into action an instinct that cannot lawfully be satisfied save under certain limited conditions—are more or less sinful, according to the degree of the excitation. Modesty as regards women's dress is subject to variations within limits according to time or place, but chastity never admits of the slightest exception.

The sins of sex are classified as internal (thoughts) and external; the external sins are according to or against nature. A sin is against nature if generation cannot follow. Thus simple fornication, in itself, is less of a sin than onanism in marriage. Birth control is inherently evil because it subordinates generation to pleasure, contrary to the order intended by nature.

Although the Church holds virginity to be superior to marriage, if virginity is chosen in order to live more nearly the life of Christ, Catholicity has always upheld the sacredness of sex when properly used in marriage. The only trace of emotion I have ever found in the hundreds of articles in the *Summa Theologica* is this answer of Aquinas to the question: "Whether the Marriage Act Is Lawful?"

"Yes—against that foul heresy and madness, according to which corruptible things were created by an evil God." (*Op. cit.*, III, q. 42, art. iii) The Angelic Doctor was referring to

118

the Albigensian heresy, with which the Church waged relentless war.

The necessity of controlling the sex instinct, however, has given rise to much that is familiar in Catholic practice. The prohibition of the eating of meat on Friday, the Lenten fasts, the prominence given to bodily mortifications, all aim largely at creating the self-discipline that will say No to unlawful urges.

What Is the Catholic Stand on Sex Education?

The principle is that this information should be given, but only when and as needed, and that the training of the will is far more important than the mere imparting of knowledge. Pius XI made this clear in *Divini Illius,* December 31, 1929:

"Far too common is the error of those who . . . falsely imagine they can forearm youth against the dangers of sensuality by purely natural means. . . .

"In this extremely delicate matter, if, all things considered, some private instruction is found necessary and opportune, from those who hold from God the commission to teach . . . it is of the highest importance that a good father, while discussing with his son a matter so delicate, should be well on his guard and not descend to details. . . . Otherwise it may happen that instead of extinguishing this fire, he unwittingly stirs or kindles it in the simple and tender heart of the child. Speaking generally, during the period of childhood, it suffices to employ those remedies that produce the double effect of opening the door to the virtue of purity and closing the door upon vice." (Paulist Press translation)

There is nothing, generally speaking, in the Ten Commandments that is not intended for all men. Hence a Catholic doctor is expected not to give out birth-control information; a Catholic druggist, not to sell contraceptives; a Catholic theater operator, not to exhibit indecent pictures, etc. Conversely, Catholics may use their rights as citizens to see that non-Catholic cinema operators, news vendors, doctors (in Catholic hospitals), etc., do not facilitate the transgression of the natural law. What is against the natural law is against the good of society.

Justice and Rights

This division of moral theology comprises the largest section on the Ten Commandments, and includes the multitudinous problems connected with ownership, exchange, contracts, injury to property, and restitution; the obligations of buyer and seller, of employer and employed, and so on. Sometimes these questions involve delicate considerations on every side, but all are solved from this one principle: that whatever is given must receive an equal or proportionate return. Otherwise restitution is called for. This is the principle of commutative justice, the virtue that requires us to render to each what is his own.

There are other forms of justice, which do not maintain the absolute equality of the thing to be received. Such are distributive justice, which inclines the government of the community to distribute benefits and burdens according to merits or means, and legal justice, which binds the citizen to obey the laws, pay his taxes, and treat his fellow citizens in a manner that will conduce to the general welfare. The rule of both legal and distributive justice is the common good. An employer violates legal justice if he practices racial discrimination in his employment practices, and a community commits a sin against distributive justice by segregation laws, oppressive taxation, and by unreasonable monopolies, as in education. The violation of distributive justice implicit in the Barden Federal Aid to Education Bill of 1949 was the reason Catholics opposed it so bitterly, as they oppose all laws giving exclusive educational benefits to those parents who happen to find it convenient to send their children to one type of school. Catholics are taxed to support the public educational system; they do not object to that, it is but legal justice to pay these taxes. But they save the state billions in taxes by operating their own schools, and they get no consideration from the state for this public service. They can no more accept this condition than they can declare black white.

The field of legal, distributive, and commutative justice covers almost all the relations, outside the family and the Church, that man can have with man. The teachings of Catholic moral theology in these matters are marked on the one hand by a scrupulous concern that justice be done and on the other hand by the realization that in this world absolute certainty is often unattainable. Hence frequent recourse must be had to the moral system of what is called "probabilism," or the doctrine that when there is an insoluble doubt as to an obligation it is permissible to act on a solid probability, even though there may be a greater probability the other way.

Probabilism simply follows common-sense rules, which are taken for granted by all educated people. One of these rules is that no one is to be presumed guilty unless his guilt has been reasonably proved. Thus a jury will not send a man to his death unless there is no reasonable doubt as to his guilt, even though the weight of the evidence points to the murder.

Another rule of probabilism is that in a doubt the one in possession has the better case. For example, there is reasonable doubt that I have paid a bill, and also reasonable doubt that I have not paid it. I am in possession; and, provided it was not my fault that the doubt about the payment of the bill arose, I can presume in favor of myself.

Whenever someone's safety is at stake, one may not go by probabilities. A pharmacist may not, for example, sell a customer a bottle that he suspects may contain poison, even though it is far more probable that it does not. A hunter may not shoot when there is even one chance in ten that the target is a man and not a deer.

Moral theology in the Catholic concept is both a strict and a humane thing.

A Church founded and inspired by God must have a constant concern that justice be done. This explains the insistence on social justice, which runs through the great encyclicals, like *Rerum Novarum* (1891) and *Quadragesimo Anno* (1931), and the pastoral letters of the Hierarchies of various countries, such as, for example, the American Bishops' pastoral of 1919, and many since. Before the *Rerum Novarum* of Leo XIII, it was taken for granted in the ruling sectors of business and government that labor was a commodity and that there was no necessity to pay a living family wage. That encyclical, and *Quadragesimo Anno,* which followed it up, did more than any other document to raise the wage level in all countries, particularly in America and the British Commonwealth. These documents simply apply the Catholic doctrines on legal and distributive justice.

On the other hand, the Church has always upheld private property. On November 9, 1846, about 2 years before Marx and Engels published the *Communist Manifesto,* Pius IX declared the doctrine of Communism to be contrary to the natural law, so that, "once admitted, all rights, property, and even human society itself would be destroyed." The Church was the first to condemn Communism as we know it today.

What Is the Church's Attitude Toward the Welfare State?

The Church has always taught that the right of private property involves a social responsibility. Property is limited by the obligations of both justice and charity. It is limited by the obligation of justice, for every man has a right to the necessaries of life and can enforce that claim on his fellows.

121

Those who are in extreme need, so as to be in danger of death if they receive no food or shelter, have a right in justice to receive, or even to take (without violence), what is necessary for their support. This is not theft but the application of the principle that God's gifts were intended for all. Thus moralists teach that an overpopulated country, unable to support itself with dignity, can allow its nationals to occupy, peacefully, vacant land needed for their support, and defend themselves against attack by those who pursue a dog-in-the-manger policy.

As regards the state, however, moral theology is clear in its position that it should regulate and encourage, and not dominate or absorb. It is against the nature of Catholicity, against its teachings on the natural law, to look with equanimity on domination by the state in matters that should be within the domain of voluntary (not necessarily private) action. Thus in January, 1955, Bishop Antonio Zapliain of the Canary Islands issued a pastoral letter sharply attacking the Spanish government's control of the trade unions. Almost the same day a Catholic paper in Paraguay was confiscated because it contained an editorial demanding that unions be free of police control.

The state can place some limits on private property for the common good, but it does not have the right to levy taxes so heavy that they would destroy private property and sap initiative. The intervention of the state is right and needful whenever great damage has been done to the common good or to the rights of individual classes, which can be remedied or prevented in no other way. Thus most Catholics were hearty in their support of the New Deal program of the 1930's, which was animated by the Social Encyclicals of Leo XIII and Pius XI. Nevertheless, whatever their politics, all Catholics must agree with Leo XIII when he declared in *Rerum Novarum:* "The laws should undertake no more, and go no farther, than the solution of problems or the removal of the danger demands."

What Is the Catholic Position on Gambling?

Gambling or wagering is treated in the moral theology manuals under the head of "aleatory contracts," those whose object is an outcome that is more or less uncertain. Gaming is simply a form of aleatory contract, which in itself is justifiable under the proper conditions; namely, that the gambler stake only his superfluous wealth, such as is not needed for the support of his family or for the discharge of his obligations of justice or charity; that no positive deception be used;

and that there be a proportion between the chances of winning and the amount stacked. Wherever the civil law prohibits organized gaming it is binding in conscience.

Catholic moralists discountenance heavy gaming and betting, even when it cannot be called immoral in itself. Of betting Father Adolphe Tanquerey, S.J., gives this judgment:

"By all means to be avoided is the ready habit of betting, especially when the stakes are high, since nothing turns men away from good hard labor more than this, and nothing leads so surely to overdrinking. This is especially true of betting on horse races. . . . Nevertheless, if the betting is done rarely, for a good motive, e.g., of relaxation . . . and the stakes are low, it is not unlawful in itself." He makes the same criticism of lottery games. (*Synopsis Theologiae Moralis*, III, NN. 911–913)

Bingo games, which are usually held to raise money for charity, and do not ordinarily breed a habit of improvidence or prodigality, are not generally condemned by Catholics in this country and England, though it is admitted that they may be abused. In the United States the bingo issue has become a trial of strength between Catholics and organized Protestants, or at least is represented as such. It is difficult to avoid the conclusion that Protestant organizations that put through anti-bingo laws are not so much concerned with the common good as asserting their will over the Catholic community.

It is most unlikely that anti-bingo zealots have ever considered that the moral theology of Catholicity places stock-market speculation, along with the Lloyds' type of insurance, in the same classification. What applies for one activity often as not applies for the other. Reckless speculation on the New York Stock Exchange, more than any other single immediate cause, brought on the great Depression of 1929–1939.

Moral Concepts Are Not Manufactured

I have gone to this length in reviewing Catholic moral doctrine, whose treasures I have hardly hinted at, because I want again to enforce on my readers the fact that Catholic moral principles are not arbitrary rules, which come out of Rome, and which have no more validity than the teachings of a sect. Moral doctrine is not manufactured, it is not the product of decree; it is elaborated from principles that are changeless.

Often you hear it said by the enemies of the Church that truth, for a Catholic, is whatever the Holy Office tells him, or that when a Catholic is in doubt on any point of morals he waits for a reply from one of the Roman Congregations. Dismiss from your mind any such thought. Questions are indeed asked of the Holy Office, the Congregation of Rites, or the Sacred Penitentiary, and answers are given—but like as not the reply will be: "Consult the approved authors."

On very rare occasions the Pope or one of the Congregations will make a decision that is somewhat out of line with what moral authors of repute have thought permissible. An example is Pius XII's statement that books for the married intimately describing the sex act are not lawful, even if they counsel nothing against nature. But in general no Catholic reasonably well instructed in his religion is ever surprised at any statement on moral questions that comes out of the Vatican. When Pius XI issued his *Casti Connubii,* condemning birth control, some non-Catholics honestly thought that this was a judgment that the Pope could make or not make or make in the reverse direction. Catholics, however, understood.

The reader who has been following me in this chapter will note the absence of peculiarity about any of the laws of Catholic morality. "Catholic morality" is in fact a misleading term, for moral theology is primarily the interpretation of the natural law, and the natural law is above any religious division. The natural law, however, is certainly *catholic,* and as such must be the particular concern of the Church Universal to uphold.

The spirit of morality is contained in these words of Pius XII, addressing the World Medical Federation, September 30, 1954: "What, in the last instance, is established by man," the Pontiff said, "a man can, in the last instance, suppress. . . . This contradicts the constancy of human nature, the constancy of its destination and its finality; it contradicts also the absolute and imprescriptible character of its essential needs. . . . The absolute character of the demands of morality stands, whether man heeds them or not. Moral duty does not depend on the pleasure of man. Only moral action is his affair."

Chapter 15

The Church Sanctifying

THE CHURCH exists to sanctify men. All her infallibility, all her incomparable teaching authority and the majesty and wisdom of her government converge in this one end. It is the very definition of the Church that she is the union of humanity with Christ. He gave Himself to her, so that she enjoys His own infallibility and dispenses the means whereby His inexhaustible sanctity is channeled down to men.

Christ could—indeed, does—give His graces to all men, even without being asked. No one but receives some help from Him. But it is Catholic teaching that He has ordained certain visible means through which His grace ordinarily flows. These are the seven sacraments, which, in the sentient phrase of St. Thomas Aquinas, are Christ's Passion applied to man.

What Is a Sacrament?

A sacrament is the sign of something sacred insofar as it produces a grace merited by Christ. This sign not only signifies but in some way actually causes grace, in the same way as the spittle and dust that Jesus Christ applied to the eyes of the blind man restored his sight. The sacraments are in fact simply acts of Christ continuing His healing activity on this earth. Thus when the minister moves water on the head of the candidate for Baptism and says: "I baptize thee in the name of the Father, and of the Son, and of the Holy Spirit," it is the water thus determined by the words of a minister who acts in the name of the Church that causes the removal of the ancient stain of original sin and makes the person a member of the Church. This it does by virtue of the promises of Christ, who is the minister-in-chief of all the sacraments.

As has been noted many times, even by non-Catholics like Goethe, the seven sacraments are so many limbs on which man's whole individual and social life is hung. Distributed throughout all life, they remind one of Shakespeare's seven ages of man:

To physical birth corresponds Baptism, which ushers in spiritual life; to spiritual growth corresponds Confirmation, which is the sacrament that gives spiritual strength to growing years, to fit the young Christian for the battles he must fight for his faith and against sin. Man must be always recruiting his strength; hence we have the Eucharist, in which Our Lord Himself is given to eat.

Man may fall sick in two ways, spiritually and bodily. For spiritual sickness is given the sacrament of Penance, whereby man recovers the grace he lost by offending God. For bodily sickness there is Extreme Unction, which is a sacrament only for those in danger of death, with the purpose of cleansing them from whatever of sin remains in them.

As the sacraments of the individual replenish spiritual life, or give it where it is not, the social sacraments, Holy Orders and Matrimony, replenish the life of the community; Holy Orders, by supplying those who will rule it for its spiritual good; Matrimony, by bringing into being new citizens for heaven.

Christ instituted the sacraments immediately, not through the Apostles or the Church, which merely has their custodianship. This is attested by both Scripture and earliest Tradition. In the New Testament we find the direct intervention of Christ in the sacraments either stated or strongly intimated in the following passages: Baptism (John iii, 5; Matt. xxviii, 19); Confirmation (Acts viii, 14; xix, 6); the Eucharist (John vi, 1–72; Matt. xxvi, 26–29; Mark xiv, 22–25; Luke xxii, 15–20; I Cor. xi, 23–25); Penance (John xx, 21–23); Extreme Unction (James v, 13–15); Holy Orders (Luke xxii, 19); I Cor. xi, 26); Matrimony (Matt. xix, 4–9; Eph. v, 20–32).

The sacraments all produce grace for a certain state or stage in life. Thus Matrimony imparts a grace that enables the couple to be loyal partners and good parents. Baptism not only wipes away sin prior to Baptism but gives the helps whereby one is enabled to be a good Christian. The sacraments do not depend for this effect on the dispositions of minister or recipient, save accidentally. The minister must have at least the intention of doing what the Church does; the recipient must be in a state of grace, i.e., free from serious sin, or he will obstruct the grace he receives, add to his sin, and in some cases make the sacrament worthless. An infant may receive the sanctifying grace of Baptism, but a man of reason will receive more or less benefit from all the sacraments the better is his disposition.

Three sacraments also produce what is called a *character*, a spiritual reality imprinted on the soul, which gives to it the power to receive or bestow on others things pertaining to divine worship. The sacramental character is a participation of the priesthood of Christ, beginning with that impressed in Baptism, which admits one into the Christian community; in Confirmation, the character makes one a soldier of Christ; it reaches its fullness in Holy Orders, which confer on the priest the power to say Mass and dispense the instruments of sanctification. This doctrine of the character illustrates once again the hierarchical nature of Catholicity. Rulers are distinguished from ruled, and yet the ruled have some beginnings of the power of the ruler.

What Is Baptism?

Baptism is the sacrament whereby, through the moving in some way of water on the head, with the utterance of the determining words, "I baptize thee in the name of the Father," etc., a human being is freed from original sin and all sin committed prior to Baptism and made a member of the Church. Baptism, like the other sacraments, belongs to the Church. The Church does not recognize other sacraments than her own. Every non-Catholic minister who baptizes validly baptizes in the name of the Church, though he be ignorant of what she is.

Baptism is the one absolutely indispensable sacrament for all men. Without some form of it no one can be saved. Through it one is made capable of receiving the other sacraments.

What Is the Baptism of Desire?

An implicit desire for Baptism, which is included in a general purpose of keeping all the commandments of God, is sufficient in one who does not know the law of Baptism. This teaching is based on the words of Christ: "If anyone love me . . . We will come to him and make Our abode with him." (John xiv, 21–23) Another way, much less frequent, by which Baptism of water can be supplied is Baptism of blood, or martyrdom suffered freely for Christ.

What of infants who die without the saving waters? The great majority of Catholic theologians through the ages have taught that they go to a place of perfect happiness called the Limbo of the Children. But this happiness was not that for which they were destined; it is a natural happiness merely, and is not blessed by the vision of God face to face.

Who Are Saved Outside the Church?

The Church is absolutely necessary for salvation in the same way as Baptism of water is the door to the Church.

We are to be saved socially, by obedience to a visible Church, which can speak with God's voice. If God had meant to rule men directly, by means of individual illumination, He would have clearly announced that purpose. On the contrary, we hear nothing of such a thing, and find that He established a Church with the power to bind and loose. Therefore all must have at least the intention of joining it, should its necessity become evident.

A chapter from American history may make clearer what is meant by belonging to the Church "in desire." During the Civil War the federal government operated on the theory that the seceding states never were out of the Union; its citizens, albeit in rebellion, remained United States citizens.

Suppose the Confederacy had won the war, but its sovereignty went unrecognized. All babies born into it would be legally federal citizens, and they could not be accused even technically of being in rebellion against Washington until, after growing up, they violated, in entire good faith, some federal law. These people would stand to the United States as Protestants stand to the Church. They would not be part of the United States but they would not be foreigners either; they would bear a special relation to the United States.

Suppose again that during this period of unrecognized sovereignty a foreigner should come to the Confederate States and be naturalized. Such naturalization would not be recognized by the United States, but these foreigners too would enjoy a special relation to the United States.

If now the Confederate States were to return to the Union, a reasonable government would distinguish between those who were in good faith and those who were in bad faith. The former would not be punished. All the legal acts that they did while they were in technical rebellion would retain their effect. Native-born Southerners would be in the position of baptized non-Catholics relatively to the Church, and the naturalized Southerners would be like non-Christians who have the Baptism of desire.

As our hypothetical Southerners did not receive all the benefits of United States citizenship while they were under Confederate dominion, so those who remain out of the Church are without certain advantages, principally the entire number of sacraments, which Catholics possess. Nevertheless, if they are in good faith they can be saved, not as Lutherans, not as Jews, not as pagans, but according to the Catholicity they unconsciously possess.

St. Thomas taught in many places a theory that many

theologians question but which has its probabilities; namely, that every child, on reaching the age of reason, chooses whether to accept or reject his last end, and thus if he should die at that instant his soul would be either saved or lost. Be that as it may, it is certain that God calls all men to salvation.

Who Can Receive the Sacraments?

Anyone can and, if he recognizes its necessity, should receive the sacrament of Baptism. If he is an adult he must desire this, at least by means of some signs that indicate such a desire. The Church never allows a sacrament to be conferred on anyone capable of reason without his consent, even though it might be conjectured on general principles that he would desire Baptism if he had its necessity explained to him. Faith is an act of the intellect commanded by the will, which the Church always respects. For the other sacraments, Baptism is also required. In the case of a dying non-Catholic who has given some signs of wanting to accept the Church, the sacraments of Extreme Unction may be conditionally conferred.

For the sacrament of Matrimony the recipients are a baptized man or woman (Catholic or not), who is free to enter that state. For the sacrament of Holy Orders it is a baptized male.

Who Administer the Sacraments?

The minister of any sacrament is one who performs the sacramental rite and thus confers it on men. There are two classes of ministers: one is the ordinary or solemn minister, who has been consecrated for the purpose of dispensing the sacraments as part of his office; the other is the extraordinary minister, or the minister of necessity. In Baptism, anyone, even an unbeliever, who seriously intends to do what the Church does, can, and in necessity should, baptize. In Matrimony it is always the marrying couple who are the ministers; the priest merely officiates. For the other sacraments the minister is always one who has been raised to the priesthood or episcopate. Only a Bishop is the ordinary minister of Confirmation or of Holy Orders, though in the former case he can empower a priest to administer the sacrament.

In many of the Oriental schismatic churches, such as the Greek Orthodox Church or Russian Orthodox Church, the Catholic Church recognizes valid Holy Orders and other sacraments besides Baptism and Matrimony. Anglican ministers, however, are not recognized as priests.

What Is the Eucharist?

"The Church of God has nothing more worthy, nothing more holy and wondrous than the sacrament of the Eucharist, for in it is contained the chief and greatest gift of God— Christ Our Lord, the Author and Fount of all grace and sanctity." So speaks the Roman Ritual, which regulates the rites of the Latin Church.

The Eucharist (literally, "thanksgiving") is both sacrament and sacrifice: sacrament insofar as Christ's body is given us to eat under the accidents of bread and wine; sacrifice insofar as Christ is offered up under these accidents for our salvation in an unbloody repetition of the sacrifice of Calvary.

The Eucharist was instituted in the Last Supper, wherein Christ said: "This is my body, which is being given for you" (Luke xxii, 19). "This is my blood of the new covenant, which is being shed for many unto the forgiveness of sins" (Matt. xxvi, 28).

According to St. Paul (I Cor. xi, 23–24), the Eucharist was being celebrated by the year 57, not as a human and novel rite but as a sacred ceremony instituted by Christ Himself in commemoration of His death.

Because of the words of Our Lord in John vi, we believe that Christ's glorified body is really present on the altar after consecration and under the accidents of bread and wine. Accidents are those incomplete beings, like extension, quantity, taste, color, smell, etc., which must have a subject to inhere in and cannot exist by themselves. According to the doctrine of Transubstantiation as expounded by St. Thomas, God, the primary cause of all things, exempts the accident of extension from the necessity of inhering in a substance, and the other accidents inhere in this extensive quantity. Christ's Body is hidden under these accidents after the manner of substance. Substance, which is an object of the intellect and not of the senses, is that which exists in itself and requires no subject to exist in. Substance, like nature, for which it is another name, is indifferent to place. Hence there is no contradiction in the fact that Christ's Body, though in its height and breadth and depth is only in heaven, can be really—in substance—in millions of places. A common point of comparison is the soul, which is in every part of the body, though one indivisible thing.

The accidents do not inhere in the Body of Christ, but miraculously, without a subject.

What Is the Mass?

From a time prefixed from eternity, Christ offered Himself to God on the Cross through a true and bloody sacrifice. But He instituted, in the Last Supper, a sacrifice to represent and continue the bloody sacrifice, which was to apply its merits to men. This unbloody sacrifice we call the Mass.

The consecration of the bread and wine is a sacrifice insofar as it effects a mystical separation between the body and blood of Christ by separately placing the sacrament of the body and the sacrament of the blood. The words of the priest in consecration: "This is My Body . . ." and "This is My Blood," since they express a separation of Body and Blood, are conceived as a knife severing the blood from the flesh.

The Mass is offered not only as an act of worship but also to obtain all spiritual and temporal benefits and to avert the divine wrath—to apply, in fact, the merits of the sacrifice of the Cross. It is the culmination of all sacrifices. The Mass has changed through the centuries, like the Church itself, but only in accidentals. No part of it but what recalls the past, no essential part of it but what was spoken or acted by Christ.

Why Is Latin Used in the Mass?

The Mass is said in some eight languages or dialects by Catholics of the Eastern Rites. Latin was not introduced into the Mass in Rome itself until the late second century. The Holy See will never force the surrender of the ancient Eastern liturgies. But the great body of Catholics use Latin in the liturgy, and it is doubtful, despite the desires of some Catholics, that the Holy See will ever permit, as a general rule, any substantial part of the Mass to be replaced by the vernacular.

The Mass must not be judged like private prayers, which a person must understand in order to express his thoughts or feelings to God. In a sense it is less the prayer of the people than that of the priest, who usually says it in too low a voice to be heard. The retention of Latin is a magnificent affirmation that our beliefs are those of antiquity; we pray as our fathers prayed because we believe as they believed. The fixity of language helps impress this fact.

It is wrong, moreover, to suppose that Latin is gibberish to the people. Every Catholic knows and loves the words before the distribution of Communion: *Domine, non sum dignus,* "O Lord, I am not worthy"; and the other key words, pronounced in an audible voice, the *Dominus vobiscum, orate Fratres, ecce, Agnus Dei.* He is not ignorant of the meaning of the *O Salutaris Hostia,* the magnificent Latin hymn of St.

Thomas sung before the exposed Host. English is inferior to Latin as a language of liturgical song.

But, regardless of language, the Eucharist is the great sacrament of Catholic unity. Black men and white go up to the Communion rail together. Everywhere you go, no matter what the Rite, from the Orient to the West, you will hear the story of the Last Supper, which precedes the act of Consecration; everywhere you will find the prayer of the celebrant: "The Lord be with you," and the response of the faithful: "And with thy spirit." Everywhere is the Holy, Holy, Holy, taken from Isaias, which begins the solemn part of the Mass; everywhere the Our Father chanted by the priest.

The Mass, like the priest's Breviary, changes from day to day and according to the ecclesiastical seasons of Pentecost, Advent, Epiphany, Lent, and Easter. Like the Breviary also, a large part of it is taken from the Scriptures, notably the Psalms, the Gospels, and the Epistles, and the remaining language is strongly colored by the Bible.

What Is Penance?

Penance is the great court of the Church. The little box, like a telephone booth, into which the Catholic slips on Saturday nights or feast-day eves brings him before God's justice more closely than he will ever come before death. Here, as nowhere else, one feels the power of the words: "Whatever thou shalt bind on earth shall be bound in heaven, and whatever thou shalt loose on earth shall be loosed in heaven." (Matt. xvi, 19)

In this tiny courtroom of the confessional the priest acts as the judge and the penitent as both accuser and culprit. "Bless me, Father, for I have sinned," the penitent begins, and then, after telling how long it has been since he was last to Confession, begins the recital of his sins, being just detailed enough to give each classification, or species, of sin. Thus it would not be enough to confess a sin against the Sixth Commandment, but it is necessary to indicate, in chaste language, the particular kind of sin committed—impure thoughts, impure desires (and the person desired, man or woman, married or single), birth control, fornication, and all the other classes of lust.

The number of sins must also be confessed as nearly as possible. All the circumstances that change the nature and species of the sin must be told—the married state, in the case of sexual sins; the relation of the person offended, in matters of piety or justice; and, in matters of justice, also the amount of damage done or whether the debt was relatively great or small.

Besides the faithful and entire confession of at least all grave sins, it is necessary that the penitent have a sincere sorrow for and detestation of sin committed, together with the firm purpose of not sinning in the future.

The confessional, when frequently resorted to, greatly discourages sins. Those who commit the same mortal sin time after time do not usually have the habit of Confession. The confessional, which is a court in miniature, composes quarrels and dissensions, reconciles enemies, and urges the observance of all laws, human and divine.

The continuous existence of Confession is one of the greatest proofs I know of the divine character of the Church. Other communions talk of instituting something like it, but they do not, and they could not, insist on the clear and faithful avowal of all serious sins as does the Church. Even the Oriental schisms, which have valid Penance, are not nearly so strict in this department.

The priest, I think, never reveals his character so clearly as when he is in the confessional, unless it is while saying Mass. My most intimate friend is a priest, full of boyishness and humorous flights of fancy. But when I confess to him, immediately the judicial dignity of the keys descends upon him. He listens to my tale of sin in a kindly way, as priests are wont to do, but always with the consciousness that He is standing in the room of Christ. Immediately afterward, the Confession will be as if it had never been.

Non-Catholics and some Catholics, too, wonder what the reaction of the priest will be after he has heard some peculiarly shameful sin. The priest will probably hear at some time in his life about every sin catalogued in the moral theology manuals, and they are all listed there. It is too much to say, as it is sometimes, that priests are never shocked or never use sharp language to their penitents. But this rarely happens— with truly miraculous rarity, considering the trying nature of Confession. It takes up hours of the priest's time in work that demands the utmost concentration.

As a matter of fact, no well-informed Catholic is easily shocked. The very nature of his religion, with its emphasis on grace and its teaching of the difficulty—nay, the practical impossibility—of long continuance in the right course without a special help from God, does not dispose him to any high degree of confidence in the sinlessness of anyone else, even when the appearances are favorable. He knows that there is no sin into which even the most careful liver cannot fall once he becomes overconfident, neglects the sacraments, and gives in to pride.

The Confessional Seal

No body of professional men have kept the secrets confided to them more faithfully than have priests. No law is stricter in the Church than that which forbids the confessor to give even the remotest hint of anything he has heard in the confessional. This law admits no exception—no evil and no good can cause it to cease, whether before or after the death of the penitent. The confessor may not speak to the penitent outside Confession of what he has learned from Confession without the penitent's free and express permission. I personally have observed no change of demeanor—not the slightest—in my priest friend after I have disclosed the seamy side of my life to him. Surely this would be impossible without a special assistance of grace.

On the basis of knowledge gained in Confession, a confessor may not discharge a housekeeper whom he knows only from Confession to be dishonest. He may not even omit a Mass if he knows from Confession that plots are being laid against him, or that the wine he uses for Mass has been poisoned. He may command the penitent to give him permission to use this knowledge; if the penitent refuses, the seal must be kept.

There have been but few historical cases of the violation of the confessional seal, even as recorded of renegade priests. I heard of one such unfortunate man who in mockery walked into a baker's shop and there consecrated all the bread; but I personally have never heard of a single priest, however unworthy, who disclosed what he had learned in the sacred tribunal.

Catholics differ widely in virtue, as they differ in politics; but what they do not differ in is the seriousness with which they take the sacraments, particularly Penance. Although I know some Catholics have written differently, I believe very few—almost none—are the people who will knowingly go to Confession without the intention of revealing a serious sin on their consciences. The *Register* receives letters all the time from correspondents—mostly women, but not infrequently men—who for some reason or other, usually an invalid marriage, have not been to Confession or Communion for years and yet never miss a Mass or a Novena. They know it is worse than useless to go to Confession as long as they have not given up their sin. And so they remain in hope.

Chapter 16

Clergy and Religious

Cleric is the generic name given to all those who have been set aside by the Church by special consecration or ordination for the government of the faithful. The sacrament by which this is done is called Holy Orders, or simply Order.

There are three divinely instituted Orders in the Church, those of minister (deacon), priest, and Bishop. The deaconship is nowadays found only in the seminaries, where it is conferred on men beginning their last year in theology. Therefore there are only two Orders that the layman wanting to understand the organization of the Church need bear in mind, the priesthood and the Episcopate.

The priesthood is distinguished by the fact that it confers a right over the physical Body of Christ, or the power to consecrate the bread and wine at Mass and change them into Christ's real Body and Blood. The priest who is consecrated Bishop receives in addition to this power of Order, which he already has, the power of jurisdiction, which means that he has the right to rule both priests and people and delegate to the priests certain powers.

It is the Bishops who came first in the Church in the order of time, as they come first in the order of dignity. To them, and to them alone, was given the power, in the Last Supper, of consecrating the Body and Blood of Christ: "Do this in remembrance of Me." (Luke xxii, 19) By these words Christ appointed the Apostles alone as priests. Afterward, the power of forgiving sins was conferred on them alone, when, following His Resurrection, Christ breathed on the Apostles and said: "Receive the Holy Spirit; whose sins you shall forgive, they are forgiven them, and whose sins you shall retain they are retained." (John xx, 22)

But the priesthood, like the sacrifice of the New Law, was to be perpetual; hence the Apostles appointed other ministers through an external visible rite, the laying on of hands, mentioned in Acts vi, 6; xiii, 3; and in Timothy, First Epistle, iv, 14; Second Epistle, i, 6. To them alone belonged the office of ruling the Church (Acts xx, 28), of dispensing the mysteries or sacraments (I Cor. iv, 1), and of offering gifts and sacrifices (Heb. v, 1). The Bishops alone have full priestly power. Priests of the second rank (called in the early Church, presbyters) are ordained by the Bishops and assigned their duties under him. They are what are called "priests" today.

The Bishop is not a simple delegate of the Pope, but holds his office by divine right. Although he is appointed by the Sovereign Pontiff, and the exercise of his office can be suspended by him, the power of Order he receives cannot be lost. In fact, the character impressed on the souls of deacon, priest, and Bishop is so indelible that one who receives it can never again become a layman, although he may be deprived of priestly functions.

The Bishop has broad powers of administration for his diocese, including the admission of members of the clergy to his diocese, the erection or suppression of parishes, and the appointment of ecclesiastical offices. The Bishop can proclaim ecclesiastical penalties, such as excommunication. He must control the religious instruction of the laity and that given in all seminaries and schools in his diocese. This extends even to public schools, as regards the instruction given to Catholic children.

Obedience to the Bishop has always been regarded as one of the marks of the Catholic mind. "No one can remain united to Christ when he acts against the Bishops of Christ." declared St. Cyprian (d. 258), in his book, *De Unitate, 17.*

Priests hold office under the Bishops. A pastor, who rules a parish, is not sovereign in his territory, but must obey episcopal laws. Except in danger of death, no priests may validly administer the sacrament of Penance except with the authorization of the Bishop. There are two broad divisions of the clergy, secular and regular (or religious). Religious priests are those who take the three vows of poverty, chastity, and obedience in some religious order or congregation. Secular priests do not take the vows, and their lives are regulated only by canon law. In certain minor particulars the regular priest is exempt from episcopal jurisdiction, but he is subject to the local Bishop insofar as the episcopal office and the organization of the Church demand it.

Most ecclesiastical legislation is concerned with the clergy and with religious orders or congregations of men and women. The priest is bound to lead a more holy life than the laity, must continue his clerical studies even after ordination, give reverence and obedience to his Bishop, lead a chaste single life, recite the Breviary every day, wear a garb in accordance with the customs of the country and the regulations of his Bishop, and refrain from all amusements and callings unbecoming to his state.

The danger of scandal besets the priest far more than it does the layman. Accordingly, canon law has laid down minute regulations for his conduct. The clergy may not engage in tavern or store keeping, indulge in games where wagers are made (unless this is done sparingly and all scandal is precluded); they may not bear arms save from justified fear; enter taverns and similar places; or engage in noisy hunting (can. 138). They may not attend theatrical exhibitions, dances, and performances that detract from the dignity of the clerical state (can. 140). They may not voluntarily do military service. They may own stocks and bonds, but may not engage in commercial transactions. Medicine and surgery and legal avocations are debarred to them without permission. A cleric may not run for the office of Senator or Representative without the permission of his Bishop (can. 139). For the United States, the Third Plenary Council of Baltimore forbids priests to meddle in political affairs, unless an essential moral principle is at stake (such as would be the absolute necessity of fighting a politician of Communist leanings).

The care that the Church takes in accepting recruits to the priesthood may be seen in the various irregularities and impediments, some of which by no means imply a stigma, which she has erected against certain classes of men. These include illegitimate birth, bodily defects that make it unbecoming to say Mass or which excite derision, epilepsy and insanity, even after they have been cured, successive marriage at least twice, the receipt of the death sentence, being born of baptized non-Catholic parents as long as the parents remain outside the Church, and several others that are more obvious.

No other religious minister in the world must undergo a longer and more careful period of training than the Catholic priest. In the seminaries the student must have, besides religious instruction, an accurate knowledge of Latin and the vernacular before he can begin his philosophy course, which lasts at least two years. The theological course must last four years, and include, besides dogmatic and moral theology, the study of the Scriptures, Church history, canon law, liturgy, sacred eloquence, and ecclesiastical chant (can. 1365).

The word *cleric* comes from the Greek *kleros*, meaning "lot" or "allotment." A priest is one set apart. His character and office do not depend on the election of the faithful but on the laying on of hands of the Bishop, who traces his line of succession back to the Apostles, who, in turn, received this power from Christ. He has a power no one else has in the Church, that of bringing grace down from heaven through his administration of the sacraments.

Although priests can and do act, speak, and talk in many things just like laymen, they are almost bodily distinguished by the character, or seal, that is impressed on their souls at ordination. In the *Register* office, where three of them work, they doff their Roman collars and clerical vest; yet I have observed few Catholics who met them for the first time who could not recognize that they were priests, despite the absence of all outward signs.

What Is the Religious Life?

Catholicity, being a religion that looks to the end of man, has a lively sense of vocation. It teaches that there are three main states in life: the clerical state, the religious state, and the lay state. The religious state should not be confused with Holy Orders or the clerical state, although some men in the religious state may be priests. Both men and women may be "religious," and a large block of canon law is devoted to regulating the conditions for their admission to and government in religious orders or congregations.

The religious state is founded on the call Christ gave to certain souls to do something above the Commandments—to follow the counsels of perfection. The young man or woman who joins an order has some sense of following this call, and this is called a "vocation." It need not, and ordinarily does not, involve any clearly defined experience. It suffices to have a desire to serve God in the most perfect way, or to have a feeling that one can best save one's soul in the religious state.

For religious a period of trial, called the postulancy, ordinarily leads up to the novitiate, which begins with the reception of the religious garb. The novitiate lasts a whole year, during which time the novice may freely leave the society or be dismissed for good reason by the superior.

At the end of the novitiate, religious profession is made. This is defined as a contract, whereby a Catholic surrenders himself to a lawfully approved religious institute by pronouncing the vows of poverty, chastity, and obedience, which are accepted in the name of the Church by the institute itself. (Arregui, *Summarium*, N. 493)

All religious are bound by force of their profession to strive after the perfection of their state by the observance of the vows and rules of the institute; to lead a common life, even in respect to food, clothing, and furniture; and to continue in their state, unless there is a just cause for leaving it, which must be approved by their superiors. (*Ibid.*, N. 498)

Canon 595 prescribes that the superiors see that their subjects attend Mass daily, make a daily meditation on some religious subject, confess at least once a week, and receive Communion frequently.

The vow of poverty forbids every independent act of ownership by individual religious, such as the disposition of material things in a way other than the superior intends. The vow of chastity forbids the slightest thought or look in the direction of impurity. It is protected by the law of enclosure, which in general forbids persons of the opposite sex to enter a specified area. The vow of obedience does not bind the religious to do anything against the rule (unless the superior can set it aside), anything above the rule (unless the superior or circumstances so direct), or anything beneath the rule.

Orders and congregations innumerable have come into existence, particularly in the past four centuries. They retain an age-old rule but continually adapt themselves to new conditions, with that power of meeting changed conditions which is one of the marks of the Perennial Religion.

Chapter 17

The Church and Matrimony

MATRIMONY, writes St. Thomas, stands in the last place among the sacraments because it has in it the least element of spirituality. But from the point of view of signification, i.e., of the union between Christ and the Church that it represents, it outranks them all. (*Summa*, III, q. 65, art. ii, ad 1; art. iii, ad 4)

The Church herself is married; she is married to Christ: "Husbands, love your wives, just as Christ also loved the Church, and delivered Himself up for her, that He might sanctify her. . . ." (Eph, v, 25 et seq.) Women who take their vows in the religious orders wear bridal veils and are called "brides of Christ." The Catholic doctrine that the Church is the Mystical Body of Christ indicates more than mere symbolism; it expresses the ineffable union of Christ with the Christian body subject to Him, which, though it can never be fully explained in this life, is a union that is infinitely closer than that which exists between, say, the president of a commercial company and his partners or employees. Its closest parallel is marriage, in which two become one flesh.

Matrimony is both a contract and a sacrament. The sacrament of Matrimony is the marriage contract enriched by the sacramental power.

As a contract, Matrimony is defined as a lawful agreement between a man and a woman, which confers on them the mutual and perpetual right both to the generation and rearing of offspring and to the fellowship of a common life.

As a sacrament, Matrimony is defined as the lawfully given, reciprocal consent of the contracting parties, in virtue of which grace is conferred on the spouses to enable them properly to perform the duties of the married state. (Tanquerey, *Brevior*, N. 1222)

Matrimony is both natural and sacramental. Natural marriage is that contracted according to law or custom between two unbaptized persons. Sacramental marriage is that contracted between any two persons who are baptized.

For unbaptized persons the state can lay down certain impediments, which make its contraction unlawful or even invalid. For baptized persons, Catholic or not, this power has been given by God to the Church. But neither Church nor state can touch the essence of Matrimony, can make a marriage, once validly contracted, no marriage. Of marriage both natural and sacramental God alone is the Author and He alone can make exceptions in it. A grasp of that fact could save many complaints against the Church, which, if written down, could be measured by the square mile.

First take marriage as a natural contract, subject to the natural law. It is not like any other contract, where one party says to the other: "This thing is yours." In marriage both parties say: "*I* (meaning my person) am yours." The end of this contract, as determined by nature, is primarily the procreation and rearing of children, and secondarily the alleviating of concupiscence and the mutual help of man and woman, who are by nature so constituted that each complements the other, as if they were needed to make one whole.

Hence marriage by nature is indissoluble. Divorce prevents the primary end of marriage from being fully obtained. For the child in order to be properly reared needs the help of both parents, not only the gentle love of its mother but also the stern authority and prudence of its father. The completion of this upbringing requires the lengthy and, indeed, lasting union of the spouses, since before the education of all the children is completed, the spouses will as a rule be no longer capable of marrying again. (Tanquerey, *Brevior*, N. 1241)

The children of broken marriages are often brought up

without a father's or a mother's care, and the lopsided emotional development that follows often leads to twisted lives and mental illness. It is no accident that, as the divorce rate has risen, so has the number of people treated for mental illness.

A further fact is that if marriage is a dissoluble contract, then it is not an equal contract, as all contracts must be. It is not equal as regards the children, for, whatever arrangements are made, the children after divorce cannot belong wholly to either one parent or the other. The parents thus lose something of themselves, something for which they married and without which marriage would never have been instituted.

Moreover, the equality of the contract is almost never preserved as regards the wife. For, though the man loses little or nothing of his dignity and can easily enter a new union, a woman who is divorced after many years has almost no hope of a new marriage, at the very time in which she is most in need of the aid and protection of a husband. (Tanquerey, *op. cit.*, N. 1242) In insisting on the indissolubility of marriage the Catholic Church has done infinitely more for women's rights than all the feminists who ever lived.

Catholic moral theology, of course, readily recognizes that in some cases a dissolution of marriage and remarriage would be for the happiness of all concerned. But the law takes no account of particular cases, but of the common good. In those severely limited exceptions in which the Church concedes the dissolution of the marriage contract, the ecclesiastical authority, which is the final judge in these cases, must approve.

I shall deal with these exceptions later. Here it is important to state that God Himself can make exceptions in the indissolubility of marriage, just as He permitted divorce and polygamy in the Old Testament. Even God cannot make an exception in the primary law of nature, without which the end of creation absolutely cannot be obtained. Thus He could not permit polyandry, whereby one woman has several husbands, for this makes practically impossible either the procreation or the proper upbringing of children. But He could, and did, permit polygyny and divorce (under certain conditions). Under either of these two systems it is possible to generate and educate children, though not so perfectly as in monogamous marriage. God, who can control the bad effects, can make these exceptions for a higher end.

According to the words of the Council of Trent (session

24, D. 969), the natural indissolubility of the marriage bond was pronounced by the first parent of the human race on the inspiration of the Divine Spirit: "Wherefore a man shall leave father and mother, and shall cleave to his wife; and they shall be two in one flesh"; (Gen. ii, 24) and Christ recalled natural marriage to its original stability in the words: "What God has joined together, let no man put asunder." (Matt. xix, 6)

It cannot be demonstratively proved from Scripture that Matrimony is a sacrament. This is one of the points of doctrine which, like the identity of the inspired Scriptures, must depend on Tradition and the teaching office of the Church for its confirmation. But the sacramental nature of the marriage union is strongly intimated by Christ's presence at the marriage feast of Cana and in the words of Paul, in which he compares Matrimony with Christ's union with the Church. (Eph. v, 22–32)

This sacrament of marriage, like all the sacraments, gives the recipients the divine helps that enable them to discharge all the burdens of the married state. By Baptism the spouses already live a supernatural life. This supernatural state to which they are elevated by means of baptismal grace means that the two are adopted children of God, and God is a third party to the marriage. Hence the malice of birth control; God is told to keep out of the marital act.

Even in natural marriage the woman would owe natural subjection to her husband, because of the difference between the sexes. In supernatural marriage this obedience takes on the additional character of the subjection of the Church to Christ, of which marriage is the image. Wives owe obedience to their husbands as the Church does to Christ. Husbands must love their wives, as Christ loved the Church. As Christ protects, nourishes, purifies, sanctifies, and loves the Church, so must a husband love his wife. Christ lives in him and loves the wife with the husband's affection. The wife gives herself with complete surrender, in the knowledge that she is giving herself to Christ within her husband. (Wilkin, *Image of God in Sex,* pp. 63–65)

This supernatural significance of marriage explains in great part why the Church opposes mixed marriages. When a Catholic marries even a baptized non-Catholic, and so contracts a sacramental union, the significance of the sacrament is lost on at least the non-Catholic, who does not believe in the Church, doubts or ignores the Mystical Body, and conceives of marriage as merely natural.

Catholics and Mixed Marriages

In addition to the reason just given, the Church, in the words of canon 1060, "most severely forbids everywhere marriages between two baptized persons, one of whom is a Catholic and the other a member of a heretical or schismatical sect."

The Baltimore Catechism No. 2, intended for grade-school children, gives the reasons, "because mixed marriages often bring about family discord, loss of faith on the part of the Catholic, and neglect of the religious training of the children." (N. 300)

Even when a dispensation is secured, the marriages of Catholic and Protestant lack the pomp with which the Church surrounds those of two Catholics. There is no nuptial Mass and the wedding usually takes place in the rectory, although the Bishop may allow it to be performed in church.

Before the dispensation is obtained the law of the Church (can. 1061, par. 1, 2) requires two promises: (a) the non-Catholic party must promise that he will not interfere with the Catholic party's religion; (b) both parties must promise that all children will be reared in the Catholic faith. There are frequently other promises that must be signed, but this depends on the regulations of the local Bishop. Such promises run pretty much the same way in most American dioceses.

That the non-Catholic may better understand what he is getting into, he is commonly required in United States dioceses to take a course of six or more prenuptial instructions in the purpose and nature of the Catholic Church; and main points of doctrine and worship, such as the veneration of saints and images, the Holy Eucharist, the Mass, Confession, indulgences, purgatory, Extreme Unction, the laws of the Church, and the duties of the married state.

A national study conducted in the years 1932–1941 by the Bishops' Committee on Mixed Marriages disclosed that in this country about 30 per cent of the marriages of Catholics are with those not of their faith. Some 30 per cent of Catholics in mixed marriages lose their faith. The chances for the breakup of mixed marriages are twice as great as for Catholic marriages. In from 70 to 80 per cent of mixed marriages there is good faith and the promises are kept. From 30 to 40 per cent of all mixed marriages result in conversion of the non-Catholic party. Separation and divorce figures are higher in mixed than in Catholic marriages. (Mihanovich, Schnepp, and Thomas, *A Guide to Catholic Marriage*, pp. 161–168)

Hence the reluctance of the Church to allow mixed marriages has sound basis, although admittedly there is scant hope of reducing their number in a country like our own. Non-Catholic religions sometimes take wholly unreasonable umbrage at the disabilities the Church applies to mixed marriages; they consider it aloofness and arrogance, and "retaliate" by urging their members not to marry Catholics.

Again I must say that the Church is *jealous*, not *envious*. The Church has the whole teaching and truth of Christ; therefore she cannot be envious. Spite or arrogance or clannishness has no more to do with Catholic marriage discipline than it has with Catholic dogma. It is simply a case of believing you have the truth and acting accordingly.

The Impediments of Marriage

The Church does not legislate for the marriages of the nonbaptized, save in the cases in which such a person contracts marriage with a nonbaptized person. But even for the nonbaptized the Church (according to Catholic theology) has the right to lay down impediments to marriage. According to the Code (can. 1038, par. 1): "To declare authoritatively when the divine law forbids or invalidates a marriage belongs to the supreme authority of the Church." The impediments determined by the Church in the Code of Canon Law follow:

Making marriage illicit, but not invalid, are three impediments: certain vows of chastity, mixed religion (between Catholic and baptized non-Catholic), and legal adoption, if the state declares that this bars but does not void marriage.

Against a valid marriage there lie thirteen impediments: insufficient age, impotence, an already existing marriage, disparity of cult (marriage between a Catholic and a nonbaptized person), Sacred Orders, blood relationship, affinity (relationship by marriage), public propriety (in relation to the marriages of a man and woman who have lived together in concubinage with the blood relatives of their partner), spiritual relationship (godmother, godson, etc), abduction or force, crime (adultery or conjugicide with an attempted marriage or a promise of marriage), solemn religious profession, and legal adoption, if the civil law voids the marriage of such persons.

From one of these impediments, namely impotence, not even God could dispense. Also of the natural law, from which the Church cannot dispense, is blood relationship in the direct line (e.g., grandmother and grandson) or in the first degree of the collateral line (brother-sister). The Pope does not in fact dispense from public conjugicide committed in order to enter marriage, or in the impediment of the Episcopal Order. Very rarely does he dispense in abduction, insufficient age, a solemn vow or Sacred Order, at least of the priesthood. Only a little less rarely does he dispense when there is question of the marriage of uncle and niece, or one who has been ordained to the deaconship or sub-deaconship.

Apparent Divorce in the Catholic Church

Whenever a celebrity (usually a movie star) obtains a civil divorce and marries in the Church, the *Register* can expect perhaps a score of letters, ranging from genuine puzzlement to the innuendo that money talks. No annulment is granted by the Church's matrimonial courts. At most the court finds that a marriage never existed in the first place.

Most often those Catholics whose previous marriages were void were married outside the Church. Catholics must be married before a priest, even when only one party to the marriage is Catholic. Otherwise, their marriage is null. Non-Catholics, even if baptized, are not bound to this form, and hence their marriages are valid, unless there is some impediment voiding the marriage. When there is such an impediment it is usually the bond of a still-existing marriage. Very frequently in a Catholic editor's mail is the query asking whether some non-Catholic who has been divorced can be married in the Church. If two baptized non-Catholics marry, their marriage is recognized as indissoluble unless an impediment intervenes, or there is a case of the Pauline Privilege or a related case, and this does not happen too often.

As regards Catholics, next to an attempted (and not real) marriage before a justice of the peace or a non-Catholic minister, the most frequent reasons why matrimonial courts declare the previous marriage illusory are lack of consent (owing to some degree of force or ignorance) and probably also unsuspected impotence prior to the marriage, or else an agreement whereby the parties precluded the right to each other's bodies except at such times, or in such a manner, that children could not be brought forth. This would be against the primary end of marriage.

Every year a Catholic paper will publish statistics from the Rota, the supreme matrimonial court of appeal of the

Church, showing that money played absolutely no part in the findings of nullity.

In an address to the Pope in an audience granted by His Holiness to the judges and officers of the Rota on October 29, 1947, Monsignor Julien, the dean of the tribunal, emphasized that out of 833 cases of nullity examined during the preceding ten years (833 itself is a significantly low number!), the Rota rejected 498 and accepted 335. Of these 335, 183 cases (or 54 per cent) were handled free because of poverty. This means that poverty does not hurt the case, if it is a good one, and that lawyers' fees have no influence on the declaration of nullity. (*Enciclopedia Apologetica,* p. 1157)

The Marconis, the Marlboroughs, and the Havers are good copy; the obscure are not. Hence only celebrities become known as people who entered a marriage invalid in the eyes of the Church.

In both the lower matrimonial courts of the Church and those of highest appeal, the Church is in fact not directly interested in the litigants themselves. She is interested in the facts of the case. Of all the courts of the world, I believe that only those of the Church have an officer to defend the marriage itself. He is called the *defensor vinculi,* the defender of the bond, and must be summoned in all cases dealing with the nullity of marriage (can. 1967). His position is neither that of plaintiff nor of defendant. He fights to uphold the validity of the marriage by trying to show the deficiency of the proofs put in evidence against it. So eager is the Church to get at the truth, and nothing but the truth, that she even waives certain legal formalities in order to better attain this end. (Woywood, *A Practical Commentary on the Code of Canon Law,* II, p. 341)

When Is Real Divorce Recognized by the Church?

The Church claims no power to dissolve marriage on her own authority, but only on that given her by God. There are two principal cases in which God has done this.

(1) A sacramental marriage that has been contracted, but not consummated, can be dissolved upon the solemn religious profession of one of the spouses; or, for grave reason, can be dispensed from by the Sovereign Pontiff.

(2) Marriage when contracted and consummated between two unbaptized persons can be dissolved under certain definite conditions, if, while one spouse remains unbaptized, the other is converted to the Faith.

The authority for the first dissolution is based on Tradition, divinely given to the Apostles and traceable to the early centuries.

The authority for the second dissolution is based on the words of St. Paul (I Cor. vii, 12–15), declaring it to be permitted by God for a converted Christian to proceed to a new marriage if his infidel partner would not live with him, or not live in peace, that is, one who seeks to draw the Christian into sin or brings up the children in a non-Christian manner. This is called the "Pauline Privilege," and is apt to be an involved case.

In the case of a ratified but nonconsummated marriage and that of the privilege of the Faith, the Sovereign Pontiff is commonly deemed to dispense by virtue of the broad power of the keys, whereby he exercises authority over the human will and can permit an act of the will by which an obligation of the natural law was induced in a particular case to be changed or retracted, whereupon the obligation itself ceases in the individual. But, because the obligation is contracted with respect to God, the act of the human will that induced the obligation cannot be changed or retracted at will but only with the consent of God. Hence when, for good reason, the Sovereign Pontiff dispenses in these cases, he is simply declaring that God consents to this change of the will. (Noldin, *Theologiae Moralis*, I, N. 117)

Marriage in the Catholic view, like anything else that is fundamental, is both simple and complicated. But the complications should not puzzle anyone who understands the principle that marriage was ordained by God for men, in view of the conditions of human nature. Marriage, like the state and Church, exists independently of human will. It is for men to conform themselves to the laws of marriage, not marriage to conform itself to the whims of men.

Chapter 18

The Church Perennial

THE miraculous thing about the Church is not her great age but her perennial vigor. It is this that the Vatican Council noted as "a great and irrefragable testimony of her divine mission." (Denz., 1794) Only the Church of Rome remains fixed and immutable in all essentials after many centuries, whereas other religions—nay, other civilizations—have undergone many evolutions. When the Chinese Empire was overthrown in 1912, no one regarded the event as portentous. The "changeless East" had been changing every generation, and in some respects was more unstable than the West.

But of the Catholic Church, and of her only, can it be said that she exhibits all the characteristics of life and growth without sacrificing her identity. The Vatican Council, far from denying this growth, affirms it: "With the advance of age or of time, the understandings and wisdom of one and all—of the entire Church as well as of the individual—may grow and progress much and mightily, but only in the proper direction; namely, in the same dogma, in the same sense, and in the same assertion." (Denz. 1809)

At the beginning of this century, a great rationalist Church historian, Adolf Harnack, expressed admirably what the Vatican Council meant. "The Roman Church," he wrote, "is the most comprehensive and the vastest, the most complicated and yet at the same time the most uniform structure, which, as far as we know, history has produced. All the powers of the human mind and soul, and all the elemental forces at mankind's disposal have had a hand in creating it. . . .

"In its organization this Church possesses a faculty of adapting itself to the course of history such as no other Church possesses; it always remains the same old Church . . . and is always becoming a new one." (*What Is Christianity?*, pp. 263–275)

Catholicity does not live its doctrines in isolation from the world; it must continually be in reaction with it. Changeless in its dogmas, it is ever changing in the men who adhere to it. Their minds develop and enlarge in the course of centuries, and as a result gain richer insights into some of the truths of faith and adjust themselves to new ways of spreading and teaching Christian truth.

It is obvious that the Church in many of its externals has changed greatly since the early centuries. There was a time when there was no canon law, no College of Cardinals, no Sacred Congregations, no Papal legations, no geographical jurisdictions of dioceses and parishes, no religious orders, no enforced celibacy of the clergy, no commandments of the Church. All that is nonessential in the sacraments and the Mass, a common liturgical language, a universal ecclesiastical fast, an Index of Forbidden Books, the works of Catholic Action, specific devotions (the Rosary, the Way of the Cross, consecration to the Sacred Heart, etc.), the sacramentals, even churches themselves—all this, I say, is of ecclesiastical, not divine institution, and can be more or less adapted, modified, reformed, or, in some cases, even abolished.

I have said that the Church is an extension of Christ on earth, humanity married to divinity. And such indeed she is, as regards her mission to guide and teach men. It was a fact that the Son of God instituted a Church to continue His work and that He endowed her with all the means of communicating sanctity. These facts were acquired once for all, and nothing can destroy them. If the Church had ever forgotten this, she would have disqualified herself forever. Her doctrine must be today what it was yesterday and must be at the end what it was in the beginning. Divine truth is a deposit, committed to the Church; it is not a patrimony of which she can dispose at will. All that has been said by Christ, either directly or indirectly, through the Apostles, must be affirmed once for all in the precise sense in which it was said. No addition is possible, no substantial subtraction or alteration is thinkable.

And yet the Church, because she is made up of men, is both sinful and sinning—holy in her saints, sinful in her sinners, and at times one and at other times the other, in the same man. There have been, perhaps, no more than three clearly unworthy Popes out of the 262 that have held St. Peter's Chair, but there have been some unwise Popes who were subject to the limitations of their time.

In the tenth century, for instance, there were twenty-five Pontiffs, some of whom held office for but a few months. The Papacy became a football between rival Roman families, and in two cases mere boys were thrust on the Papal throne. The French Republic has not lasted a hundred years, and yet we hear fears expressed that the frequent change of ministries in the French system will ruin the republican system. If this can be said of a temporal government which is expected to change often, what must we say of a government whose end transcends the world? How could it survive such instability? Yet survive it did.

The Papacy has had its periods of growth and decline in almost rhythmical alternation, and even in the thirteenth century, when its power was greatest, there were times when it could not make its will prevail. In the eleventh century there was danger of Bishops and priests becoming a hereditary caste and of the Church's being frozen in feudalism. The Papacy under Gregory VII (1073–1085) broke the power of feudalism over the Church, and yet Gregory himself died in exile.

The victory of Hildebrand set the stage for the glorious thirteenth century, called the most Christian in history, but even then disruptive forces were at work. Popes and Emperors, Kings and Bishops alike failed in loyalty to the ideal of a truly Christian commonwealth. The Papacy descended to the fifteenth century, at whose end Popes were looked upon by many as petty kings and not spiritual fathers, and scandals accumulated to such a degree that many persons believed that devils were in possession of the principal parts of Rome.

This decline in Papal prestige was one of the chief disposing causes of the disruption of Christendom in the early sixteenth century. Yet that century saw a succession of able and even saintly Popes, and the great Council of Trent, which reaffirmed and clarified old doctrines and reformed old abuses.

In the seventeenth century an enemy appeared in the form of Gallicanism, which would have split Catholicity into various national churches. In the eighteenth century the unwise decision of Clement XIV to dissolve the Jesuits resulted in a severe blow to education and the missions. In the beginning of the nineteenth century Pius VII was a prisoner of Napoleon. There followed a succession of short-lived or mediocre Popes and then the long reign of Pius IX (1846–1878), which, though unhappy in some of its relations with the world, was a period of doctrinal stability and development. It saw the definition of Papal Infallibility and the Immaculate Conception.

The accession of Leo XIII (1878–1903) brought to the seat of Christendom a consummate statesman and a man keenly alive to the political and economic needs of the world. He issued a series of brilliant encyclicals defending the Church's position in regard to modern liberties and urged the reconciliation of French Catholics with the republic. His *Rerum Novarum* (1891) laid the guidelines of industrial peace and justice.

The decade of the reign of Pope St. Pius X saw the crushing of the Church's most dangerous heresy, Modernism. Benedict XV, the war Pope, proposed a peace in 1917, which, had it been adopted, would have spared us the woes of Communism. Pius XI, in his encyclical on Atheistic Communism in 1937, outlined all the dangers and deviations of that insidious pest a decade before the fashionable commentators awoke to them. Pius XII has had a Pontificate that will go down as one of the greatest in history.

The Church has not been exempt from the vicissitudes of history. Her very catholicity demands that she be constantly facing problems and solving them. Pius XII intimated this in his famous allocution, *Ci Riesce*, to the Italian Catholic jurists December 6, 1953:

"The Church, in the fulfillment of this her mission, has always been faced, and is still faced in large measure, by the same problems that the functioning of a community of sovereign states must overcome; only she feels them more acutely, for she is obligated to the purpose of her mission, determined by her Founder Himself—a purpose that penetrates to the very depths of the spirit and heart of man. . . .

"For the Church with her mission has been, and is, confronted with men and nations of marvelous culture, and with others of almost incredible lack of civilization, and with all possible intermediate degrees—diversity of language, of philosophy, of religious belief, of national aspirations and characteristics; free peoples and enslaved peoples; peoples that have never belonged to the Church, and peoples that have been separated from her communion. The Church must live among them, and with them; she can never declare before anyone that she is 'not interested.' "

To meet the problems presented by her diffusion throughout the world and her presence in every ultimate question of mankind, the Church must be making constant adaptations. Until 1914 the influence of Europe within the government of the Church was so predominant that there seemed little exaggeration in Belloc's saying that "the Faith is Europe and Europe is the Faith." Since then there has been a great revolution. Full recognition has been given to the fact that Western Europe is today no longer the leader of the world. Churchmen from every distant land—not only from the Americas and Australia, but from India, Armenia, Syria, and China—now sit in the College of Cardinals, the Senate of the Church.

The need of reclaiming the European proletariat, in great part lost to the Church in the nineteenth century, has led to all sorts of experiments in France, particularly the Priest-Worker movement, whereby priests have gone out to work in factories in order to establish contact with their milieu. The movement got out of hand, the Priest Workers were disbanded, and a modification of the plan was introduced by Papal constitution in 1954. But experiment goes on.

It has been only since 1953 that important changes were

151

introduced into the law of fast in the United States. Before that year few in the United States thought that a day would ever come on which they could hear Mass at 6:00 P.M., and need to fast in order to receive the Eucharist only a few hours previously, instead of up to midnight of the day before, according to the former discipline. Many were genuinely shocked when they were told they could drink water after midnight at any time up to receiving Communion at a morning Mass.

The Pope himself was in advance of most of the sisterhoods when in September, 1952, he urged that their garb be more in keeping with the needs of the active life in the modern world.

The liturgy of the Church is a contemporary and living reality, and in no other field of her activity can we better observe the fact that catholicity means the retention of essentials and the elimination of nonessentials.

Before the reign of Pius X, in the first decade of this century, a habit had taken hold of the Church of regarding the reception of the Lord's Body as a reward of good conduct and not as a help thereto. The Eucharist was rarely given to children. A decree of 1905 recalled the Church to her ancient practice.

In 1948 came an Apostolic Constitution settling an age-old dispute among theologians as to just what constituted the essential matter in the ordination of a priest. In 1946 a decree gave parish priests the faculty of administering Confirmation to the dying. In the years before 1939 the Austrian dioceses had obtained the use of a ritual partly in German, partly in Latin. There followed a similar concession for nations speaking the French tongue. Permissions have also been given for the saying of certain blessings and the administration of certain sacraments in Spanish, Italian, Portuguese, and English.

And in all this the great facts of the life of worship, the sacrifice of the Mass, the sacraments, and the consecration of things for sacred use remain the same as they did in St. Paul's day.

In her reactions with world problems the Church is sometimes said to change, when in reality what happens is that she is ever trying to change the world, while adapting her tactics to new conditions. Leo XIII in his *Rerum Novarum* laid down nothing basically new in his presentation of the Church's answer to the problems of social strife and injustice. The condemnation of usury, the advocacy of trade unions and employer-employee partnership, the statement of the social purpose of wealth and the role of the state as a social regulator, the enunciation of the rules and principles governing workers' hours, wages, and associations, the reprobation of child labor and the employment of women in tasks not befitting their sex—the moral roots of all these can be found in the writings of the Fathers and the Magisterium of the Church in all ages. Only the needs of the time brought forth their closer application.

Leo XIII wrote in that very encyclical: "Age gives way to age, but the events of one century are wonderfully like those of another; for they are directed by the Providence of God, who overrules the course of history in accordance with His purposes in creating the race of man." (N. 43)

If it could ever be proved that a Pope had presented false doctrine to the Catholic world, that proof could surely be found in the matter of the marriage tie. Yet in age after age, as we ascend from the time of the Apostles, we never find the least hint of any weakening of that bond on the part of any Sovereign Pontiff, though it is true that in the first twelve centuries certain particular councils and certain prelates of the Eastern Church allowed divorce in some circumstances. Alexander VI (reigned 1492–1503) has been accused of approving the declaration of nullity of two marriages on grounds technically correct but on questionable testimony—but never did Alexander say that marriage is dissoluble, nor did he lay down any other decision not in accord with Catholic morals.

To maintain doctrine consistent over a long period of time and in many countries, we have Bishops, it is true— each one a judge in his own city—and above the Bishops there is a Sovereign—the Pope. But Popes and Bishops themselves are subject to the shifts and turns of time, however fortified they may be by the grace of office. Nothing in the millennial history of the Church shows that she has discovered some wonderful "work of human policy," such as Macaulay in his celebrated essay on Ranke's *History of the Popes* bade us study. The Church has known no golden age; she has no "increasing purpose" running through her history. Her purpose remains what it always was: the salvation of men, an end that is no different today than it was in the days of Peter, though circumstances may counsel sometimes different means to obtain it.

Nor does this doctrine, which is so consistent with itself, remain shut up in a closet, among a closed group, without action from the outer world. It is not put under the custody of ignorance, or sheltered from discussion, or embalmed in the dead past; but it mingles with all the movement of the world; it is the great ferment of history; it is set out in the midst of the most vibrant nations of civilization, exposed to all the floods of ideas, to all the heats of passion, to all the assaults of brute force that break upon the world.

And yet this polity penetrating all the polities of the world till the end of time has been preserved from the one thing that could bring about its fall—essential contradiction or inconsistency in its purpose or constitution. Subject to the ordinary action of history, it escapes its decay.

This is so true that it is remarkable that even in matters which do not engage the Church's infallibility, even in matters of discipline, the mind of the Church has run remarkably constant through the ages. This was nobly instanced in Pius XII's address to the Sixth International Congress of Penal Law, October 3, 1953:

"It is about 1100 years," said the Pope, "since the great Pope Nicholas I, in the year 866, replied in the following manner to the question of a nation that had just come into contact with Christianity (*Nicolai primi responsa ad consulta Bulgarorum, cap.* LXXXVI, 13 Nov., 866—*Mon. Germ. Hist.,* Epp. Tom. VI, p. 595):

" 'If a thief or a bandit is caught, and denies what is imputed to him, you say among you that the judge should beat him on the head with blows and pierce his sides with iron spikes, until he speaks the truth. That, neither divine nor human law admits.' " Just a year later Pius XII affirmed the same abhorrence of torture before the Twenty-third General Assembly of the International Police Commission, October 15, 1954.

True, in the thirteenth century the Papal Inquisition, following the usual custom, allowed the use of torture to be applied only once and in a way that would not imperil life or limb. In appraising such a policy, and indeed the whole Inquisition, we must recall that the heresies in question were looked upon as endangering the very life of the community and that the common sentiment of the day demanded the severe searching out and punishment of heretics. Nevertheless, it is not in the Inquisition of the Middle Ages that we must look for the Church's spirit, but in statements like those of Nicholas I of the ninth century and Pius XII of the twentieth. *They* are the typical ones.

Chapter 19

The Church Expanding

HOWEVER the Church may alter in certain of its externals throughout history, a few facts remain constant. Among these are constant expansion, or tendency to expand, and constant fruitfulness in the production of holy men and women.

Every feature of growth and virility noted by Macaulay in 1840 is with the Catholic Church today. She still has to confront "hostile kings"—in numbers and power greater than ever before. She still outnumbers all other Christian bodies combined. Her numbers are thrice what they were then, although the world's population has scarcely more than doubled.

Our records, unsatisfactory though they are, suffice to show that by 1800 Christians were in all the provinces of the Empire and in Mesopotamia. "Already," writes Kenneth Latourette, "the main outlines of that organization were appearing which attempted to give concrete reality to the vision of an inclusive community, which seems to have been present in Christianity from the beginning." (*The First Five Centuries,* p. 85)

"Never in the history of the race," Latourette continues, "has this record ever quite been equalled. Never in so short a time has any other religious faith, or, for that matter, any other set of ideas, religious, political, or economic, without the aid of physical force or of social or cultural prestige achieved so commanding a position in such an important culture." (*Ibid.,* p. 112)

True, this growth has not been always constant. In the Middle Ages Catholics have been estimated at 22 per cent of the entire world; after the Reformation the figure sank to 16 per cent; it then grew slowly to 18 per cent, and is now about 19 per cent, an increase of about one per cent over the year 1883. (*La Croix,* Sept. 9, 1954, p.3)

In the eleventh century the Oriental Churches were largely lost to Catholicity by the Oriental schism, and from about the fifth century onward there were many Oriental Christians who retained a validly ordained clergy and sacraments but were not in communion with the Holy See. The Nes-

155

torians at one time numbered 80,000,000. Today they have less than 100,000.

In the time of Constantine Christians numbered at least 5,000,000; they were 15,000,000 when Clovis' Baptism began the Catholic history of the French nation; under the Empire of Charlemagne the figure rose to 30,000,000. In Luther's time the Catholic population was 100,000,000; three centuries later it was 200,000,000. Under Pius X, at the turn of the century, Catholics were estimated at 300,000,000. Today 472,000,000 is perhaps not an exaggerated estimate. (See *Register*, July 4, 1954, p. 1, and *Osservatore Romano*, June 30–July 1, 1950, *Leggenda e Storia*.)

But even more than this almost arithmetical ratio of increase is the expansion of the Church into all quarters of dominant civilization in every age. In the third century she penetrated beyond the confines of the Roman Empire, and Armenia became the first Christian state. (Latourette, *First Five Centuries*, p. 105) In the next century she established herself in Ethiopia, and the lands around the Black Sea. The 400's saw the conversion of Scotland and Ireland, and before the 500's were over Augustine had struck the death blow to paganism in England. Bavaria, Switzerland, and Belgium fell under the power of the Cross in the seventh century; in the eighth, most of Germany was converted. In the 800's the Church spread to the Scandinavian Peninsula and to Russia and Bulgaria.

Poland, Hungary, Finland, and Prussia became Catholic. In the thirteenth century the Franciscan Friar Odoric made his way over the great Asiatic heartland to find, in the port towns of Fuhkeen and Schwan Chow, houses of his order already established, and when he reached Peking he met Archbishop John of Monte Corvino, the incumbent of the first see of Cathay.

In the next century Franciscans and Dominicans were baptizing thousands in India, and Franciscans were translating the New Testament into the vernacular in Eastern China. Before the death of the first Archbishop of Peking there were 30,000 Christians in the city of the Great Khan, and Mass was being celebrated in the Tatar tongue. (Walsh, *Thirteenth, Greatest of Centuries*, pp. 410–412; McSorley, *Outline History of the Church by Centuries*, p. 466; *Dictionnaire théologique*, art. "Langues liturgiques," col. 2584)

The sixteenth century saw the expansion of the Church to Mexico, South America, and the Philippines. Before the persecution of the early seventeenth century Japan had thrice as many Catholics as she has today. In the seventeenth century the Jesuits were powers in the Ming and Manchu courts of China, and seemed on the way to converting the nation. They gave that land, on a plane of rationality, what Communism seems to be giving it today on a plane of irrationality. (Toynbee, *The World and the West,* p. 63)

Catholicity today has the following distribution percentage-wise: Asia, 2.5; Europe, 39; the Americas, 56; Africa, 9; Oceania, 21. The only countries in which it has practically no existence are Afghanistan, Arabia, Greenland, Tibet, and Outer Mongolia. (*Register,* July 4, 1954, col. 1)

No other proselyting force in history has had this constant tendency to convert and assimilate peoples of the most varied backgrounds, without absorbing their identities. In the Soviet Union the most important posts are given to White Russians, and native "Presidents" of the Tartar republics of Central Asia are show-window. As late as the early twentieth century the Anglican Church had found it impractical to consecrate native-born Australian Bishops in a country of Anglican dominance for a century.

The Church and the Saints

The Church in every age—from the days of the first martyr, St. Stephen, and those of Polycarp, who was martyred in 155—has had an instinct to hold up men and women of heroic virtues as patterns of the Christian life. If she did not produce these persons, whom we call saints, she would be defective in one of her four essential notes, that of holiness.

To be a saint canonized by the Church one must be far more than a good man, like George Washington or John Wesley. One must perform "virtuous actions with uncommon promptitude, ease, and pleasure, from supernatural motives and without human reasoning, with self-abnegation and full control over natural inclination." (Benedict XIV in his treatise on beatification and canonization, quoted in *The New Catholic Dictionary*, art. "Heroic Virtue") He or she must be eminent in the practice of the social or cardinal virtues of prudence, justice, temperance, and fortitude, and in the theological virtues of faith, hope, and charity. The principal requirement in the process for the beatification and canonization of "servants of God" is to prove that they practiced these virtues in the extraordinary or heroic manner thus defined by Benedict XIV.

Heroic virtue means, to put it concretely, that a St. Peter Claver will never in a long lifetime spent among the slave Negroes of Venezuela shrink from tending the most loathsome sufferers, precisely because he sees in them the children of God. It means that a St. Therese of Lisieux will, during her short life, practice scrupulously the doing of the simple, unexciting things that her ardent nature would ordinarily rebel at doing. No one pretends that heroic virtue among Catholics is common, but every Catholic, or non-Catholic, who has a wide circle of acquaintance in Catholicity will know of some man or woman, not necessarily a monk or nun or priest, who, he is sure, is practicing the virtues in a heroic degree nearly all of the time.

The Church takes infinite pains in canonizing her saints, and that is why, since the reign of Sixtus V (1585–1590) when the present procedure of canonization was introduced, only 205 persons have received this honor. But the number of uncanonized saints will run into the thousands and tens of thousands, if indeed they will not at the last judgment be reckoned in the millions.

Anti-Catholics, like Paul Blanshard, speak sneeringly of the "manufacture" of a saint, but the process of canonization, and that of beatification which precedes it, has nothing mechanical in it. No less than 142 canons of the Church's Code deal with these procedures (can. 1999–2141). The superiors of religious orders are strictly forbidden to influence their subjects to conceal the faults of a servant of God, and speak only of his good characteristics, or vice versa (can. 2026). Catholicity hungers for the truth, and would cease to be Catholicity should it ever cease to have that single-souled devotion.

Chapter 20

Tolerance in the Church

"GREAT MINDS need elbow room," wrote John Henry Newman (who became a Cardinal) in his *Idea of a University*. "And so indeed do lesser minds, and all minds." Before Catholic truth has reached the stage of definition considerable play is allowed to speculation.

The Holy Virgin, for instance, has always been regarded in the Church as "full of grace." And yet this fullness of grace, even at the time when belief in the Immaculate Conception had made decisive progress, did not hinder certain theologians of name, for example the celebrated Cajetan, from affirming the opposite doctrine without incurring rebuke. This would not be tolerated today, a century after the formal definition of the Immaculate Conception, but the fact that it was tolerated then shows the large place the Church gives to the action of the mind when a truth is not yet so clear as to be defined dogma, or proximate to definition.

Anyone who picks up a Latin manual of moral or dogmatic theology will be struck by the number of times an assertion is qualified by phrases such as "according to a probable opinion," "it is believed with probability," "it is more probable that . . ." The liberty granted the Church to such opinions is more than tolerance, in fact, for tolerance normally implies something thought to be evil that is tolerated. In permitting this wide gamut of theological opinion on matters that have not reached the stage of Catholic doctrine, the Church considers them as valuable expressions of dogma, each with its own plausibility, each furthering the day when truth may be reached. Innumerable are the different explanations given, for example, of the liberty of Christ, the way in which the sacraments cause grace, the inspiration of Scripture, the reconciliation of grace with liberty and of God's foreknowledge with His will to save all men. There is, in fact, much more play of opinion within the framework of Catholicity than there is in even the most liberal non-Catholic religions, for the simple reason that there is more material to work on, it is more highly developed, and there are guidelines telling what is assured truth, what is safe, what is probable or more probable, what is rash or false.

Certain opinions, which enjoyed probability at first, later became simply tolerable, and now are not even tolerable, when the contrary opinion has assumed in the ordinary Magisterium of the Church the character of theological certainty. But the very reason these opinions pass from the status of "free" to that of "unsafe" is that men's minds have reasoned on them until the truth becomes clear. The purpose of freedom in theology is to establish truth. A good illustration of what I mean is a former theological opinion that Christ's soul was ignorant of something. A decree of the Holy Office of June 5, 1918, confirmed that the doctrine of a universal knowledge in Christ, as taught by the ancient theologians, must be called certain. But such a decision did not come until the question had been thoroughly aired in theological debate. Dogma and defined doctrine as little impede the movements of the Catholic's mind as the laws of physics impede his bodily movements.

In his notable essay, "Christianity and Scientific Investigation," Cardinal Newman came out nobly for freedom of inquiry in a Catholic university, not for the purpose of confusing immature minds in professorial lectures, still less for calling into question the doctrines of faith, but in order to get at the truth more surely. "I still say that a scientific speculator or inquirer is not bound, in conducting his researches, to be every moment adjusting his course by the maxims of the schools or by popular traditions, or by those of any other science distinct from his own . . . or to be ever answering heretics and unbelievers; being confident, from the impulse of a generous faith, that, however his line of investigation may swerve now and then . . . if he lets it alone it will be sure to come home, because truth never can be contrary to truth." (*Idea of a University*, N. 7)

And then the great Churchman went on to appeal to the intellectual ferment of the high Middle Ages: "If there ever was a time when the intellect went wild, and had a licentious revel, it was at the date I speak of. When was there ever a more curious, more meddling, bolder, keener, more penetrating, more rationalistic exercise of the reason than at that time? What class of questions did that subtle, metaphysical spirit not scrutinize? What premise was allowed without examination?" (*Ibid.*, N. 5) Anyone who has ever read a work of St. Thomas or St. Bonaventure or St. Augustine, or for that matter a single textbook of dogmatic theology, such as the four volumes of Herve, or even the one little *Brevior Synopsis* of Tanquerey, will appreciate that such an accumulation of thought could never have been reached if broad freedom had not been allowed for the ideas there propounded, at least at some time in dogmatic history.

More place, of course, is accorded in the Church to practical than to doctrinal tolerance. The Church will not tolerate anything contrary to the law of God, whether it be the positive divine law or the natural law. Also, she interdicts every practice that by its nature or by reason of circumstance is connected with infidelity, idolatry heresy, or schism. She could do no other.

But even in this last point she has room for flexibility. The Chinese Rites were sternly forbidden in the seventeenth and eighteenth centuries, but allowed in a decree of December 8, 1939, when it became apparent they were of a civil and not of a religious nature.

What is more rigidly stated than this regulation of canon

1060? "The Church forbids most severely and in all countries marriage between a Catholic and an heretic, or schismatic." Yet dispensations from this law are being given all the time in the United States, not lightly, it is true, but for reasons of the general good, to avoid worse evils.

A rich field for tolerance lies in the vast area that the moral theologians call "co-operation in evil." The Church severely condemns direct co-operation in every intrinsically evil act, that is, every act that by its nature tends solely to the accomplishment of sin. But in the much more numerous acts that come under the head of "material co-operation," which do not themselves partake of the act of sin, toleration is extended according to the gravity of the reason. Often such co-operation is not merely tolerated; it is called lawful, for otherwise human existence would be impossible.

The Church in her history has often tolerated acts that she deems less perfect. For example, she allows the marriage of priests in the Oriental Rites, despite the praises she lavishes on virginity and on celibacy in the priesthood. She has tolerated bizarre customs, like that of the dancing procession of Esternach in Spain; and relics and legends of doubtful authenticity.

Here an explanation is in order. The Church can never found piety on pious frauds, but, as long as a relic or a narrative about a saint's life are not certainly false, she generally tolerates them, if they are good in themselves and further the piety of the people.

It is possible—for aught I know probable—that the pieces of wood venerated in the Church of St. Mary Major in Rome as the crib in which Jesus was laid are not authentic. But what the people venerate is not the wood but the Infant Jesus, of whom the wood, authentic or not, is a reminder and a symbol.

The Toleration of Non-Catholic Religions

Some of what I intend to say on this subject will be reserved for the final chapter. Here I want to indicate some of the historical manifestations of Catholic tolerance. St. Thomas Aquinas laid down the principles governing the question in II-IIae, q. x, art. 11 of his *Summa:* "Ought the rites of unbelievers to be tolerated?" he asks. And he replies: "Human governments must conform to the divine government, of which they are an emanation. Now, despite His infinite power and goodness, God allows in the world the existence of certain evils that he could hinder, because their suppression would involve the loss of far greater goods or even provoke far greater evils." Pius XII, in his pivotal allocution to the Italian Jurists December 6, 1953, simply recapitulated the language of St. Thomas in this matter. All Catholic thought is continuous with history and dovetails into theological principles.

Francisco Suarez (d. 1617), perhaps the greatest theologian since St. Thomas, considered every direct constraint on unbelievers, even those subject to the Christian prince, as intrinsically evil. (*De Fide*, disp. xviii, sect. iii, n. 5–11)

The Church has never approved anti-Semitism, and, when certain civil governments showed undue rigor against the Jews, they always found asylum and protection in the States of the Church. Because of anti-Semitic outrages in connection with the First Crusade, Callixtus II issued the bull *Sicut Judaeis* about the year 1120. It laid down that the Jews must not be forced to accept Baptism; nor should they be injured in life, limb, or property save by due process of law; nor should they be disturbed in their festival celebrations or obliged to render feudal service beyond what was customary. This bull was reissued or confirmed by twenty or thirty Pontiffs during the next four hundred years. (McSorley, *Outline History of the Church by Centuries*, p. 362)

Throughout history, the few attempts at coercion of non-Catholics by Catholics have come from civil rulers acting for purely political ends. They have always been opposed by the Church. Charlemagne, in his forced Baptism of the Saxons, was withstood by Alcuin; the medieval Church persistently refused to "liquidate" its Jewish problem by the simple expedient of allowing the civil arm to remove Jewish children from their parents' care to have them baptized. After the Revocation of the Edit of Nantes in 1685, the French Bishops protested against the policy of forced Communions for the Huguenots. In 1941, when, after the collapse of organized Yugoslav resistance to the Germans, the Pavelic government of Croatia issued a decree declaring that the Orthodox Church in that land was suppressed and that its members must become Latin Catholics, Archbishop Stepinac immediately, on May 8, sent a letter to his priests, in which he warned them that they must strictly observe the provisions of canon law in receiving converts into the Church: "An adult shall not be baptized except with his own knowledge and consent and after due instruction." (can. 752)

And, hardly a month later, on June 29 came the encyclical letter of Pius XII, *Mystici Corporis,* in which, in undoubted allusion to Pavelic, the Pontiff stated: "Whenever it happens, despite the invariable teaching of the Apostolic See, that anyone against his will is compelled to embrace the Catholic faith, our sense of duty demands that we condemn the act."

Catholic abhorrence of forced conversion is not a matter of policy. It coheres with the theological fact that faith is an act of the intellect under the command of the will. Since no one can force the will, no one can force another to believe. An adult who is baptized without his consent is simply not baptized according to Catholic teaching on the necessity of an intention in adult recipients of Baptism. (Denz., 411)

Once again, Catholicity is *jealous,* not *envious.* The Church is not afraid of benefiting non-Catholic religions indirectly, if so be a higher good may be obtained. She is like the true mother who before the judgment seat of Solomon declared she would give her child to a false mother rather than see it cut in two. Hence conservative English Catholics have sincerely voted for the retention of the Establishment in England, because, though they know the Anglican Church is the immediate beneficiary of such arrangement, they fear the loss of prestige that might come to religion as a whole should the Anglican Church be disestablished. Ireland, with a population of 99 per cent Catholic, freely gives subsidies to non-Catholic parents for the education of their children in their religion. Quebec, 80 per cent Catholic, is far more generous in its apportionment of funds to non-Catholic religious schools than any of the predominantly non-Catholic provinces of Canada. Were she a follower of expediency the Church would give tacit consent to the birth-control propaganda now going on in pagan India and Japan. But there she fights this thing as vigorously as she does in the United States.

No other religious body elicits so many acts of tolerance as does the Church. I am here using the word "tolerance" first in the sense of disposition to allow the existence of beliefs not one's own; and, second, of a specified allowance for error in weighing and measuring. The Church cannot tolerate *within her bosom* any doctrine or practice that is deemed unsafe to follow; but she willingly allows the tolerance of non-Catholic religions. The Magisterium permits a broad "tolerance" in theological opinion (never to be confused with dogma), because it needs to allow for error in order to get at truth. When truth is arrived at the need for this tolerance disappears.

163

Chapter 21

The Church Progressing

BECAUSE of its respect for the human intellect the Church Teaching is in some ways the most democratic of institutions, for its suffrage has the widest base—the Church Teaching even becomes at times the Church Learning. She has been learning in the past and will learn in the future, not by the acceptance of new truths, not by understanding a truth of faith in a way different from that in which it was understood by former generations, but by a more distinct understanding of the Deposit of Faith left by the Apostles.

Even a Pope, in one age, may have a less distinct knowledge of an article of faith than a child in a succeeding age. That is, a child in a later time may understand explicitly what an earlier Pope understood only implicitly, as being contained in a more general doctrine. Thus Pope Benedict XIV (1740–1758) wrote during his Pontificate, as a private theologian, that the Assumption of the Blessed Virgin was not an article of faith, for "certain passages of Scripture, which are usually adduced to establish this opinion, can be explained otherwise, nor is the tradition on this point such as suffices to raise this opinion to the rank of an article of faith." (*De Festis*, lib. ii, c. 8, n. 12 ff., quoted from Bover, *La asunción de Maria*, p. 423)

Yet, on November 1, 1950, Benedict's successor called the Assumption an article of faith, necessary for the belief of all, and adduced Scripture and Tradition in its support. Obviously, then, the Assumption, though even in 1758, when Benedict wrote this, it was not, as the Pope himself admitted, permitted to deny it, had not evolved in Catholic theology so distinctly as to make its definition practical. It can never be stressed enough that Papal infallibility is no quick and easy means of establishing truth.

Indeed, writes Herve (*Manuale Theologicae Dogmaticae*, III, N. 295), by the help of his teachers, and the prompting of the Holy Spirit, any one of the faithful who firmly adheres to the rule of faith, which is found in the perennial and authentic teaching office of the Church, can have a more perfect knowledge of dogmas than existed before. For the Bishops first define them indistinctly and later on propose them as explicit objects of faith or explain them more logically—not that the knowledge of dogmas consists solely and simply in an evolution of the Christian consciousness, but rather in a firmer and richer faith, which the faithful receive from the Church teaching under the action of the Holy Spirit, who illuminates and guides them by His gifts.

By their own efforts all Catholics can, with the exercise of study and the observance of the rules laid down by the Fathers and Doctors, derive conclusions that will add to their appreciation and knowledge of the Faith. This labor, of course, is only a preparation for progress; the Church must approve whatever conclusions are reached. Thus, for example, the Church explicitly and distinctly proclaims first the complex dogmas: Christ is God and Man; the Mother of God is the all-holy Virgin; St. Peter has primacy over the entire Church. Then she proposes the elements that make up those dogmas, to wit: there is one Person in Christ, but there are two natures, two wills, and two operations; the Blessed Virgin is immune from original sin; the Sovereign Pontiff has these rights and these duties, etc.

Three stages can be distinguished in the history of any dogma. First, the stage of implicit faith; then, the stage of hesitation and controversy, when a head of doctrine is attacked or more thoroughly studied and examined; and, finally, the stage of Catholic faith, when, after all doubt has been rejected, either by the solemn decision of the authentic teaching office of the Church or the weight of unanimous consent, it is proved with certainty that the dogma has been revealed, and it thereby becomes an explicit part of the Catholic mind and the clear teaching of the Church. In the process of elaborating the definition of dogma all Catholics have some part. In fact, the outcry of the faithful against Nestorius, who asserted that there were two Persons in the Son of God, helped not a little to define the doctrine that Mary is the Mother of God.

All men, in the teaching of Catholic faith, are in a state of pilgrimage, and consequently so is the Church. This shows how misplaced was the irony of the noted Swiss Calvinist theologian, Karl Barth, when he wrote in reply to Father Henri Danielou anent the Amsterdam Ecumenical Conference of 1948:

"At Amsterdam no Church presented itself against others as being the sole saving and infallible Church, that is, a Church that has already found within itself and by itself the answer to the questions that we posed together. In fact we faced one another as simple denominations. . . . You would not have been able to sit at our side, but could only place yourself on a visible or invisible seat, on a lofty throne above our heads. Among us poor Protestants the rich man is offensive, in the same way as is the man well filled among the starving and among pilgrims the man who has reached his goal." (*Reforme,* Oct. 23, 1948)

Fine irony, I repeat, but misplaced. The Church Teaching and the Church Learning have not reached their goal and are not well fed with justice and the fruition of all truth. The Church Militant must pursue her way and hunger for justice until the end of time. Only the Church Triumphant, in heaven, is rich. Here below she affords us certainty, whereby we may do perfectly the will of God. But she gives none of her children grounds for complacency with themselves or reasons for arrogance toward those without the fold. The virtue of theological hope, which despairs of no man's salvation and gives to no man assurance that he will be saved, is surety for that.

The Church is married to every age but is identified with none. She did not identify herself with feudalism, though she made use of it; or with the institution of kingship, though she has made alliance with kings. Nor will she accept democracy as a religion, however much Popes and Bishops and Catholic laymen may praise that political system in the temporal sphere.

The Church Expanding, the Church Sanctifying, the Church Progressing are all phases of one Church Militant. The wide scope she gives to tolerance is but a manifestation of her infinite adaptability combined with her unbending rigor.

Chapter 22

The Church Governing

IN 1954 there passed almost unnoticed the 150th anniversary of the promulgation of the Code Napoléon, upon which Napoleon himself rested half his claim to fame. Even before the nineteenth century was out, that monument of jurisprudence was beginning to be superseded by the more scientific German law. But the Code of Canon Law by which the Church is governed retains its vigor today even more than in the days of Gratian, who first codified it in the mid-twelfth century.

Canon law, in the judgment of a French jurist, René David, "constitutes as much as—nay, more than—Roman law the most gigantic attempt at unification of law that has ever been essayed in any field, however varied." (*Osservatore Romano,* Sept. 13, 1951)

Canon law in the Middle Ages was binding upon all members of the community, from king and emperor down to the lowest villein. It dealt with every conceivable aspect of medieval society—including the relationship between clerics and laity, between kings and Bishops; the protection of property; crimes and their punishment; marriage; the position of the excommunicated, the heretic, the apostate; the rights of burial, etc., besides obviously ecclesiastical matters.

This universality is no less evident in the 2,414 brief paragraphs that constitute the miracle of concision called the modern Code of Canon Law, promulgated only in 1918, but reaching in some of its precedents to the very beginning of the Church. Most of these statutes are man-made, though of venerable date in the Church. Many of them, however, only delare the natural and the positive divine law. Mere canon law is never to be confused with that which is from above, although even pure canon law is or can be gravely binding in conscience.

The Code is divided into five books. The first book comprises the general principles regulating the Church and its society. The second book gives the law for the three great divisions of people within the Church, the clergy, the religious (members of religious institutes approved by the Church), and the laity.

The third and largest book, from canons 726 to 1551, is entitled "Sacred Things." It lays down in detail all the laws regulating the administration of the sacraments, including Matrimony, which affects most of the laity and even, indirectly, non-Catholics. A second part of the same book regulates the erection and care of churches and cemeteries and ecclesiastical burial. It determines the holy days of obligation, on which all the faithful are obliged to hear Mass, and the rules for fast and abstinence from flesh meat.

Part III of the same book, regulating divine worship, specifies what honors shall be given to the saints, sacred images, and relics, and establishes the rules for the making and observance of vows and oaths. Succeeding parts cover the teaching authority of the Church and include the important canons requiring parents to send their children to Catholic schools and forbidding certain types of books. A concluding portion states the law governing the administration of parishes and ecclesiastical property.

The fourth book, called "Canonical Trials," contains the rules governing the inquiry into ecclesiastical offenses and matrimonial cases, and the complex proceedings required for the beatification or canonization of a saint.

Lastly comes the fifth book, on "Offenses and Penalties," which covers ecclesiastical punishments, such as excommunication, interdict, suspension, and the corrective and punitive penalties of Church law.

What Distinguishes Canon Law?

I have already alluded to one point in which the law of the Church is sharply different from all codes of civil states —its concision. Think of it! Governing 470,000,000 people, almost a fifth of the world, there are only 2,414 canons, the great majority expressed in one terse paragraph, though together they cover fields of the widest diversity.

Three other things distinguish Church law: humanity, reasonableness, and moral stability.

Canon 2214 is a fair illustration of the spirit of canon law, which seeks first to influence the Church's children in the forum of the conscience, and only when this is unavailing resorts to penalties:

"The Church has the innate and proper right, independent of all human authority, to punish her guilty subjects with both spiritual and temporal penalties. The admonition of the Council of Trent, Session XIII, cap. 1, shall, however, be kept in mind, from which it is clear that the Church does not favor the rash and hasty use of extremely severe penalties and censures. The Council reminds the Ordinaries to consider their subjects as children and brethren in Christ and urges them to try as long as possible, by patience and kindness, to influence them to strive after virtue and to desist from vice." (Woywood, *A Practical Commentary on the Code*, II, p. 412)

Canon law, like our Constitution, prohibits ex post facto laws (can. 10). It makes the responsibility for an offense dependent on the intention of the delinquent, or his moral accountability (can. 2199). Litigation is discouraged (can. 1925). Any of the faithful have at all times the right to denounce the offence of another for the purpose of asking for satisfaction or for justice's sake (can. 1935). In ecclesiastical criminal trials no consideration is given to denunciations that come from a professed enemy, or a vile and unworthy person, or an anonymous letter (can. 1942). Husband and wife possess equal rights and duties respecting the actions proper to married life (can. 1111).

There is no acceptance of persons in the Church—laity, clerics, Bishops, Archbishops, and Cardinals have all their rights and duties strictly determined. Only the Sovereign Pontiff is not subject to the judgments of ecclesiastical tribunals (can. 1556), but the canons have a power of direction even over him, inasmuch as the Pope must follow them for the right and honorable fulfillment of his duty. "In fact," says Herve, "the Pope would not act lawfully if he arbitrarily changed or abrogated (these laws) without any cause. For the natural and divine laws demand that the Pontiff, who by virtue of his office must procure the good of the Church, shall enforce the canons adopted for this purpose, unless conditions arise that are altogether different and new, so as to demand their abrogation or change." (*Manuale Theologicae Dogmaticae*, I, N. 502)

Canon law has a paternal quality about it. It makes a place for custom in applying the law. Unbending in principle, it has developed a system of dispensations to adapt itself, where principle is not involved, to individual situations. The Bishop is bound to conduct himself as a father, who reluctantly resorts to rigorous measures in correcting his children. Many of the punishments inflicted by Church law are "medicinal," that is, their first aim is the correction of the offender. The moral beauty of canon law is unrivaled.

But what most distinguishes the law of the Church is its command of the inmost conscience of man. The 2,414 canons of the Code represent an immense and unparalleled effort to promote virtue—nay, rather sanctity, and sometimes moral heroism. Where in any civil code can you find the like of this? "Christ the Lord Himself raised the matrimonial contract among the baptized to the dignity of a sacrament." (can. 1012) Or this? "The primary object of marriage is the procreation and upbringing of children; the secondary purpose is mutual assistance and the remedy of concupiscence. The essential qualities of marriage are unity and indissolubility." (can. 1013) In civil codes laws governing the marriage tie may be loosened or tightened as much as ten times in a century, as they have been in France, but in the Code the union remains indissoluble through the centuries.

But what most distinguishes the law of the Church is the demands it makes on its consecrated personnel. No government in the world dares demand that its officers be saints or even heroes, save exceptionally. In canon law the first of the twenty paragraphs outlining the obligations of clerics specifies that "both the interior life and the exterior behavior of the clergy must be superior to the laity and excel them by the example of virtue and good deeds." (can. 124) Priests must make a meditation of some duration each day, and a daily examination of conscience (can. 125); they must continue the study of the sacred sciences (can. 129–130); they may not marry (can. 132); they must wear a certain clerical garb (can. 135); they must abstain from all things unbecoming their state (can. 138). They must practice perfect chastity, say the hour-long Divine Office each day, and distribute all superfluous revenues from their benefices to charity (can. 1473).

Reflect on the dosage of virtue that celibacy demands of the priest, and what perpetual cloister means for the nuns! A considerable part of canon law is devoted to prescribing these great duties. If a young man receives the subdeaconship, he binds himself forever to entertain not so much as a thought against chastity; if a girl makes profession in a cloistered order, she must pass her life within convent walls, without leaving and without receiving anyone. These are heavy obligations, and yet the Church does not hesitate to make them the object of her legislation; and surprisingly her law is obeyed.

The world knows nothing like canon law. Its formation, its development, and its effects escape sociological laws.

Does the Church Claim the Right to Use Force?

I shall let a passage from the article "Immunités ecclésiastiques" in *Dictionnaire apologétique* speak on this touchy subject, which is of historical but not practical importance:

"It is not enough to judge; it is also necessary to execute the sentence, and, as all Christians are not saints, the use of force sometimes becomes necessary. The Church has therefore the right to make use of force. All the theologians teach this, and the Sovereign Pontiff has publicly affirmed it by the condemnation passed on proposition 24 of the Syllabus. . . .

"But how reconcile the exercise of this right with the constitutions of modern states, which entrust exclusively to governments the use of public force? . . . It is therefore impossible for the Church today to make use of her right. She can judge, but her decisions have validity only for Catholics of good will. She resigns herself to this necessity, without too many regrets, because today, in view of the dispositions of the greatest number of people, the use of force by ecclesiastical authority would be materially and morally impossible."

In itself, it is no more unreasonable for the Church to exercise force on her recalcitrant members than it is for the army to have its own laws, courts, and enforcement and penal system.

Aside from the recognition given to canon law as determining the nullity or validity of the marriages of Catholics, few Catholic states today enforce Church law, nor has this been demanded generally in the concordats signed with these countries. Spain, for example, by the concordat of August, 1953, makes the use of the ecclesiastical or religious garb by those clerics or religious to whom this has been denied by the ecclesiastical authorities unlawful and punishes it, upon notification of the civil government, with the same penalties that apply to those who unlawfully wear the military uniform (art. xvii). But this is hardly enforcing Church law; it is rather the maintenance of public order.

"The use of force" has a sound much worse than it will be found on analysis to bear. It is not thought tyrannical for the army, to which soldiers do not often come by their free consent, to enforce its laws by its own officers and courts and to punish them in its own way. No one, on the contrary, comes to the Church save by his free will; he makes an implicit contract with the Church to live up to its laws, and private contracts, even in a modern state, are enforced by the law. Moreover, there is no question any longer of the Church's having its own prisons and enforcement officers; that was distinctly a product of medieval times, and the system perished with those times.

The United States Supreme Court itself, in the case of Watson vs. Jones (10 U.S., 13 Wall.), ruled that whenever questions of discipline or faith or ecclesiastical rule, custom or law have been decided by the highest Church judicatories the legal tribunals must accept such decisions as final and binding. (Weywood, pp. 333–334)

Is Church Government Constitutional?

The Church has the most foolproof constitution in the world. It is impossible to be misled by it. This constitution is called the "analogy of faith," which means that no doctrine and no theory or practice of morals can be admitted if it conflicts with the deposit of revelation guarded by the Church. The Pope is as much bound by the analogy of faith as is the humblest lay Catholic.

171

Most theologians deny that a Pope could be even privately or personally a formal and contumacious heretic—Providence, they say, would not allow it. But if it should happen, he would be out of the Church, like any other contumacious heretic. (Herve, *Manuale Theologicae Dogmaticae*, I, N. 501)

Besides the one fundamental reason of special divine providence, there are many reasons why power in the Church could rarely be abused, particularly by the Sovereign Pontiffs. I have heard of Popes called immoral or simoniacal, but never tyrannical.

The Catholic Church is a hierarchical and monarchical society. It is hierarchical because its members are not of equal degree, but some have positions of authority over others. It is monarchical because supreme power is vested in one man, independently of the Bishops. By the mere fact that it is hierarchical it can never be an absolute monarchy, for under the Sovereign Pontiff are the Bishops, who are subordinate to him but are true superiors, who rule their provinces by ordinary right.

Power in the Catholic Church is of two kinds: (1) the power of Order, which transmits the faculty to sanctify souls; and (2) the power of jurisdiction, which is immediately directed to ruling the faithful in view of their attainment of eternal life. It involves the right to teach (the sacred Magisterium), the right to make laws, the right to make authoritative decisions affecting the faithful (judicial power), and the application of sanctions against transgressors (coercive power).

The power of Order does not necessarily involve the power of jurisdiction. A priest may not even validly hear Confessions without authorization from his Bishop.

In the Hierarchy of Order there are three ranks: ministers, who serve the priests; the priesthood, whose distinctive mark is power over the Body and Blood of Christ, i.e., the power to consecrate the bread and wine; and the Bishops, who have the fullness of priestly power, inasmuch as they have power, not only over the physical body of Christ but also over His Mystical Body, the Church.

There are ten actions proper to Bishops: to ordain clerics, to receive the profession of nuns, to consecrate other Bishops, to administer Confirmation, to dedicate churches, to depose clerics, to participate in Church councils, to bless the oils used in the sacraments of Confirmation and Extreme Unction, to consecrate vestments and vessels, and to make laws for their dioceses.

The power of a priest, as St. Thomas says, is surpassed by the power of a Bishop as by a power of a different kind. But the power of a Bishop is surpassed by that of the Pope as by a power of the same kind. Hence a Bishop can perform every hierarchical act that the Pope can, whereas a priest cannot perform every act that a Bishop can in conferring the sacraments, save by the Bishop's delegation.

The Pope, though in the Hierarchy of Order he is only Bishop of Rome, has direct authority over all Catholics and is subject to none. No Church council may depose him or veto his decrees. No Bishop may be chosen without his approval. He is the supreme judge in matters of faith. No ecclesiastical council may be held without his permission. No legislation, no judgment binding the whole Church may pass without his approval. He alone can form, suppress, and divide dioceses and approve new religious orders. He can inflict censures such as excommunication, and dispense from any vow.

Next to the Pope in dignity, and in hierarchy of jurisdiction, come the Cardinals. Their principal duty is to assist and advise the Pope in the details of Church administration and in deciding questions of discipline. It is the Cardinals (normally seventy in number) who elect the Pope. They are the senate of the Church.

Corresponding to the ministries of secular governments are the eleven Roman Congregations, which together with the Pope are called collectively "the Holy See," just as the king and his ministers are called the English Crown.

The most important of these bodies is the Congregation of the Holy Office, of which the Sovereign Pontiff himself is prefect, and which guards the doctrine on faith and morals. It is the final court of appeal in cases of ecclesiastical offenses. It has power to dispense from purely ecclesiastical laws against certain marriages, and examines and may forbid certain books.

Next in importance comes the Consistorial Congregation, which among other things establishes new dioceses, gives advice on the appointment of Bishops, and examines their written reports.

The Congregation of Religious has jurisdiction over religious organizations of all kinds—their government, discipline, property, and privileges. The Congregation of the Sacraments has charge of all disciplinary regulations of the seven sacraments and of dispensations from marriage impediments and questions concerning the validity of marriage and Holy Orders.

The Congregation of the Propagation of the Faith has the vast work of supervising the far-flung Catholic missions.

The Congregation of the Council has charge over the entire discipline of the Christian people and the clergy not in religious orders. It has the duty to see that the precepts of Christian life are observed.

Matters of rites and ceremonies and canonization causes come under the charge of the Congregation of Rites. The Ceremonial Congregation regulates the etiquette of the Papal Court. The Congregation for Extraordinary Affairs constitutes or divides dioceses. The Congregation of Seminaries and Universities determines the administration and curricula of educational institutions established by Church authority. The Congregation for the Oriental Church has reserved to it all affairs of any kind relating to the persons, discipline, and rites of those Catholics who are distinguished by the fact that their Mass is said in a different rite and tongue from that of Western Catholicity.

Then there are the central courts of the Church and the Papal diplomatic service. But, notwithstanding this central bureaucracy, Popes and Bishops still determine Church government. The constitution of the Church is the reverse of totalitarianism. Power is carefully distributed. In theory the Pope has tremendous powers, but in practice he seldom interferes with local Church government. If the Church were totalitarian, Bishops would be completely subordinate to Archbishops, and parish priests to Bishops. But an Archbishop has virtually no power over the Bishops of his province. The Bishops are not mere vicars of the Pope, for they have jurisdiction over their own dioceses, which is not a simple delegation.

The Bishops are not removable at will, like the functionaries of modern states. They receive their jurisdiction from the Sovereign Pontiffs, true; but, once installed, they can be removed only for canonical cause, and then only after a major canonical trial.

The Papacy, so often accused of absolutism, has always maintained the stability of the episcopate. On the contrary, immediately after severance from Rome, Bishops lose their independence. It was so in England after Henry VIII; it was so in Russia, at least after the time of Peter the Great.

The lower clergy in their turn are by no means without constitutional rights. Diocesan government is regulated by canon law. The Holy See alone has the right to dispense with that law as occasion demands, and it rarely does so. A whole block of canon law deals with the rights and duties of a pastor. An irremovable parish priest has rights that a Bishop may not override. He can indeed be removed by his Bishop for just cause, but only according to procedures laid down by canon law.

174

The Church abhors arbitrariness in government. She has constantly at heart the arrest of any tendency to domination. In all the degrees of the Hierarchy the superiors have at their sides a consultive assembly whose influence is appreciable. The Bishop must consult his diocesan synod, which must be convoked at least every ten years (can. 356), and his board of administrators as regards the administration of ecclesiastical goods (can. 1520). The Pope is assisted by his Cardinals, and, even when he does not convoke a council, he continually consults the Bishops dispersed throughout the world on important questions. Provincial councils are demanded at periodic intervals by canon law. It may be a duty for the Pope to convene an ecumenical council if exceptional dangers threaten. The superiors general of religious orders have their advisory council, and lesser superiors have theirs. This in itself is a great brake on any tendency to tyranny in the kingdom of the Church.

There are other guarantees, of an immediately human nature, which make the government of the Church the most constitutional on earth. First, there is celibacy. The rule that priests can never marry assures two things: the contact of the Hierarchy with the people and the amazing elasticity of Church government.

Since ecclesiastics can have no children of their own, the clergy must be continually recruited from elements taken from the different classes of the people; that is why the bonds of the clergy with the people are so immediate, and the Church has the advantage of a sound aristocracy, without the disadvantages of a closed caste. Even the bitterest enemies of the Church have recognized this advantage, for instance, Adolf Hitler, in his *Mein Kampf* called celibacy "the cause of the perennial freshness that activates that ancient institution."

In the second place, celibacy procures for the Church a ruling class detached from the cares and preoccupations of the family, and thus allows both Bishops and priests to remain wholly at the disposal of the people. The vast Catholic missionary enterprise, the exuberance of Catholic works of mercy would be impossible were there not in the Church heroic spirits detached from family ties. The Pope, placed in the center of the Church, is the first to feel its evils and the first to offer a remedy. This man, become the father of the faithful, has renounced in advance all other fatherhood; he will love his Church as his own inheritance, as a father loves his children.

A second guarantee of constitutionality in the administration of the Church is the mode of election of its officers. At the peak of the Hierarchy is the Supreme Pontiff, elected by a two-thirds vote of the College of Cardinals by a secret ballot, established in 1179, antedating the Australian ballot by seven centuries. The way in which the Pontiff is elected was called by the Positivist philosopher, Auguste Comte, "a masterpiece of political wisdom."

A third guarantee is the dominance in Catholicity of tradition. The Church would destroy herself if she ever reversed a single dogmatic decision, if she did not remain true to the teachings of Christ, which are her constitution. But even in those points of ecclesiastical government that are subject to change, the Church is slow in making innovations, and then she is careful to attach them in some manner to the past. Moreover, the authorities that guard tradition, the Papacy and the Episcopate, are themselves stable, and, as such, independent of opinion. Such a system offers far more guarantees of responsible government than can a strictly democratic regime, where the order of centuries can be overturned in minutes by the tyranny of a majority, and often of a determined minority.

A fourth guarantee is the age-old Catholic distinction between Church and state, which Catholicity by its very genius can never suffer to become obscured. "God," said Leo XIII, in the encyclical *Immortale Dei,* "has divided between the ecclesiastical and the civil power the task of providing for the good of the human race. The first He has set over things divine and the second over human things. Each of them is sovereign in its sphere; each of these is confined to perfectly set limits, drawn in exact conformity with its nature and its principle; each of these is therefore circumscribed within one sphere, where it can move and act in virtue of the rights that are proper to it."

The Soviet and Iron Curtain governments have been able to control the Orthodox and Protestant bodies within their territories, by inserting their own men in the governments of these bodies. They have never been able to penetrate the Catholic Hierarchies in these countries, and a decree of excommunication, most specially reserved to the Holy See, lies against "any Bishop, to whatever Rite he belongs, and with whatever dignity he be invested, who gives episcopal consecration to anyone who has not been appointed or expressly confirmed by the Holy See; and likewise those who receive consecration, even if they be constrained by grave fear, incur ipso facto the excommunication reserved in a most special manner to the Holy See." (Decree of the Holy Office of April 21, 1951)

Is it not strange that the only religious body on earth that has successfully resisted the encroachments of the civil power is constantly charged with seeking union of Church and state? So far has this been from being true that the Church in America has, on at least three occasions, resisted attempts on the part of powerful statesmen to control appointees to its high offices.

Had Benjamin Franklin had his way, Catholics, in the first days of the Republic, would have been subjected to a foreign superior, nominated by French influence and residing in France. (Guilday, *Life and Times of John Carroll,* p. 187) Theodore Roosevelt tried to have his favorite man appointed Archbishop of Manila, but Leo XIII would have none of it. (Wayman, *Cardinal O'Connell of Boston,* p. 107) Harold Ickes told of how Franklin Delano Roosevelt unsuccessfully tried to have a Cardinal appointed to his liking in the thirties. Ironically, the occasion for the proclamation of the Law of Separation of Church and State in France came when two French Bishops refused to obey a summons by Pius X to present themselves at the Holy See. The Pope's threat to censure them was described as a violation of the concordat, diplomatic relations were broken off, and the anticlerical ministry of the time decreed separation. (McSorley, p. 902) All through Church history you will find the Church fighting to resist interference with its affairs by the state, not the reverse order. Since the Church cannot by its nature allow any interference by the state it can never become a rubber stamp for autocracy like the Russian Schismatic Church.

Another, powerful guarantee against Church tyranny is the Catholic respect for the natural law. Never will the Church violate this law, or even keep silent about the need of its observance, even though from a temporal point of view this turns to her disadvantage. Recall what I have said about the Church's regard for parental rights, even of non-Catholics.

Finally, the principle of pluralism, whereby the Church encourages subordinate societies in civil life, carries over into her own organization. Nowhere in her system is there bureaucratic uniformity; everywhere there is life and fruitful variety. No other organization has so many subordinate bodies, all with a surprising degree of self-government. Far from showing herself jealous of this development of orders and congregations, the Church has encouraged them in every manner and has showered them with favors and privileges. By the law of exemption, whereby the most important orders and congregations are partially withdrawn from the authority of the Bishop, the Church has demonstrated her desire to assure them a large

177

degree of autonomy that they may better perform their work. The central power of the Church has always been the protector of the soundest liberties. (*Dictionnaire apologétique,* art. "Gouvernement ecclésiastique," passim)

The organization of the Church, wherein both rulers and subjects have their rights and duties clearly defined and delimited, is an image of the world in little. In creation, minerals, plants, animals, men, and angels are so many steps leading up to God. Now God, in the words of Aquinas, "that He might be mirrored in His works, not only as He is in Himself, but also as He acts on others, ordained that last things should be reduced and perfected by middle things, and middle things by first. And therefore, that this beauty might not be wanting to the Church, He established Order in her, so that some should . . . be made like to God in their own way, as co-operating with God, even as in the natural body some members act on others." (*Summa,* III, q. xxiv, art. 1)

The Church Universal is a mirror of the world, and each diocese, with its Bishop-Prince and his consulters and the parishes of his diocese mirrors the Church Universal. In the polity of the Church natural harmony has reached its apex.

Chapter 23

Between Principle and Policy: The Church Reacting with the World

I HAVE ENTITLED this book: *What Is Catholicity?* not *What Is a Catholic?* I am not concerned, save accidentally, to give my evaluation of the nearly half-billion people who may be called Catholics. They differ more widely than any other grouping of people in history. My intention is to present here the main principles on which these people should act or react, according to their religion. Hence in this chapter I consider irrelevant any objection based on the contrary action of those Catholics who may act or think differently from the way they should according to Catholicity.

Principle is that from which all action springs. It is a principle of Catholicity that the Church, being a sovereign society in its own sphere, is not subject to temporal society in any matter involving faith and morals. Hence a Catholic will on principle fight Communism and a state monopoly of education, to name but two examples.

Policy is concerned with the manner of carrying out principles, and, within limits, it may vary indefinitely from age to age, from country to country. It is a principle, for example, that the family—be it a Catholic family or any other—has the right to educate its children in its own way, conformably to the natural law. This means that the family may not be punished for following out this right by way of a disguised fine, in the form of paying all their taxes for one type of school and not receiving any proportional benefits for the expenditures it makes for its own type of school. The Catholic must always protest against even the modified form of state monopoly of education that obtains in the United States. That is a matter of principle. How, when, and where he will protest will be regulated by policy.

Some Popes have been incontestably wiser in policy than others. All Catholic historians today admit that the long reign of Pius IX (1846–1878) was inferior, as regards policy, to the succeeding reign of Leo XIII (1878–1903), though Pius IX, who defined the dogma of the Immaculate Conception and convoked the Vatican Council, registered the greatest advance in dogmatic theology in modern times.

Rarely do the modern Popes give expression to any view that is not intricately associated with dogma and principle. But one of the few things that can be said of all the Catholics throughout the world is that they are singularly unimpressed with the admitted opinions of their prelates, or even their Popes—if indeed it can be known that something which a Pope has said is merely an opinion and not an exercise of the office of the Church teaching.

Take Pius XII's transmission to the American government in early 1953 of an appeal to him to save the Rosenbergs from the electric chair. It is not known even today whether the Sovereign Pontiff was really putting in a plea for mercy or was merely trying to disarm European Communist and sentimentalist criticism that he was doing nothing for these persons, who were represented almost as heroes at the time, even in some conservative papers. But, whatever his intention, it is certain that he did not mean by his action to teach the Christian world. And no Catholic in America would have felt himself obligated in the slightest to desist from his demands that justice be executed against the Rosenbergs, no matter what the Pope's personal views.

No Bishop and no Pope could command Catholics to support or oppose a party or policy in which the moral or religious issue was not clear. And those who expect him to do this are almost never Catholics, although many so-called liberals are actually astonished when Catholics remain un-affected by what they consider directives from the Holy See. A good instance of this occurred in May, 1951, at the time MacArthur's discharge was shaking the United States. Alistair Cooke, the American correspondent of the *Manchester Guardian*, had the misimpression so many people have that anything you read in *Osservatore Romano* is straight from the Pope's mouth. When he read an article in that Vatican City daily that purported to back Truman against the general he wondered why Catholic Americans did not withdraw their support from MacArthur, and was shocked to think of how these Yankee Catholics disobey the Roman See!

The Vatican does, however, take sides between contending powers whenever an issue of religion is clear, and it expects Catholics throughout the world to agree with its action; and most Catholics do. Thus when Francisco Franco entered Madrid in March, 1939, Pius XII made a special radio broadcast praising those who fought in defense of civilization against the spread of atheism, referring to the attempt of the Soviets to gain control of Spain and establish a Communistic stronghold in Western Europe. He wired the generalissimo congratulations on his victory, "which we desired." (*Register*, April 4, 1939; April 9, 1939)

Catholicity never underwrites the policy of any secular ruler, even though he be a St. Louis of France. But when a Charlemagne, a Godfrey of Bouillon, or a Don Juan of Austria fights against the declared enemies of Christianity it never hesitates to support them in this, though it may and does reserve the right of criticism.

What Are the Areas in Human Affairs in Which the Church Claims Authority?

We should speak of aspects rather than of areas, since the Church admits that the spiritual often has a temporal side, in which the state is rightly concerned. Pius XI expressed this fact in his encyclical, *Ubi Arcano* (1922): "The Church does not believe that she is ever permitted to intervene without reason in the government of these earthly and purely political matters; but she is within her rights when she tries to hinder the civil power from taking occasion from its political mission to oppose, in whatever way, the superior interests that involve the eternal salvation of men, or to injure these interests by unjust laws and demands, or else to attack the divine constitution of the Church herself, or to trample under foot the sacred rights of God in human society."

Since the Church is a sovereign society for all that affects the guiding of men to their last end, and since the last end is higher than any temporal end, it is for the Church to decide what the Church may do. Otherwise she could not be an infallible teacher in matters of faith or morals.

Pius XII, in an address November 2, 1954, to 250 prelates in Rome, mentioned four aspects of human affairs in which the Church must have the final voice:

1. The ultimate powers of the state and the relations between the individual and society. The state, being concerned with man's temporal welfare, cannot decide man's final destiny, nor can it give man rights independently of God.

2. The limits to the secularization of the state and of public life and education. The state exists to protect man in his life on earth, but nothing can in the last analysis be temporarily good that is inconsistent with the laws of God. Thus a public order that completely ignores God, and forbids the Church to act upon it, is an immoral order. The school must equip the child, not only for human society but also and primarily for the divine society of heaven. Hence the school comes within the purview of the Church.

3. War, its morality, lawfulness or unlawfulness, as waged today, and whether a conscientious person may give or withhold his co-operation in it. This should be self-evident.

4. The moral relationships that bind and rule the various nations. Since nations can violate the rights of other nations and their own citizens, nations are subject to the laws of morality, and hence to the guidance or rebuke of the institution entrusted with safeguarding morality.

The following are the principal rights that the Church can and must defend in the modern world:

THE RIGHTS OF THE FAMILY—Since these rights pervade other centers of interest, they will be specified under subsequent headings.

THE RIGHTS OF EDUCATION—The school is a crossroads where meet three societies: the Church, the family, and the state. Said Pius XI in his *Christian Education of Youth:* "The subject of Christian education is the entire man, spirit joined to body in the unity of nature, with all his natural and supernatural faculties as made known by reason and revelation. That is why the religious element must penetrate even purely human instruction." This explains the prior interest of the Church in the supervision of the school.

Besides the divine right of the Church in education comes the natural right of the parents. St. Thomas advances the reason: "The child is naturally something of the father; and

181

at first is not even distinguished as to the body from its parents as long as it is contained in its mother's womb. But after it leaves the womb, before it has the use of free will, it is contained under the care of the parents, as in a kind of spiritual womb." (*Summa*, IIa-IIae, q. 10, art. 12)

Education cannot pertain to the state in the same way it pertains to the Church and the family. The function of the civil authority is to protect and foster, and not to absorb the family and the individual. The state should protect the educational rights of the child in the parents' default. But the state is never to put itself in the place of the family, but only to correct its deficiencies.

All this is in perfect accord with the Constitution of the United States. The Supreme Court has repeatedly held that the right of selecting a school belongs to the parents. A Catholic citizen of Los Angeles, William N. Webber, has appeared faithfully before the Board of Education of that city with this reminder:

"Parochial or religious schools are authorized by and required by law. They are required by law, for it is only by their means and agency that the churched citizen can secure and be assured his constitutional religious guarantees for the 'free exercise thereof.' "

As I said before, the demand of the Catholic that the state consider him (and other parents who wish to send their children to their own religious schools) is a matter of distributive justice. The issue cannot, and will not, be dropped, however long the battle. Pius XI made this clear in the encyclical, *Christian Education of Youth*, which I have so often quoted: "Let no one say that in a nation where there are different religious beliefs it is impossible to provide for public instruction otherwise than by neutral or mixed schools. In such a case it becomes the duty of the State—indeed it is the easier and more reasonable method of procedure—to leave free scope to the initiative of the Church and family, while giving them such assistance as justice demands."

The educational programs of Ireland, Holland, and Quebec, where a fair and impartial policy of aid to family or voluntary schools is pursued, are favored in Catholic thought, and wherever you do not find them perfectly upheld—whether in France, Belgium, in Argentina, Mexico, Italy, or in the United States, there you will find Catholic protests.

THE PRINCIPLE OF SUBSIDIARITY—This is a peculiarly Catholic principle, and covers a vast field of rights. It is thus stated by Pius XI in *Quadragesimo Anno:* "Just as it is wrong to take from the individual and hand over to the community what the individual can accomplish by his own initiative and enterprise, in the same way it is an injustice, a grave evil, and a disturbance of right order to transfer to a greater and higher society what can be effected by smaller and lower groups."

Subsidiarity, then, means that the lowest unit of society able to accomplish a particular function in an effective way and without detriment to the general welfare should be permitted to do so.

The principle of subsidiarity explains why, in 1954, the St. Louis and New Orleans Archdiocese officially opposed "right-to-work" laws, which would cripple legitimate labor unions. Subsidiarity acts as a buffer between an all-engrossing state and the citizen. The principle of subsidiarity, or the right to organize for legitimate ends, is often attacked by fuzzy liberals, who raise the cry, "pressure group," whenever Catholic organizations exercise their legitimate rights to protect their children and their fellow citizens against filthy prints, pictures, and cinemas. How else can citizens make their voice heard save by pressure groups?

THE RIGHTS OF LABOR AND THE INDIVIDUAL—The battle for the living and family wage and for right conditions of labor has been fought by the Church and always will be fought, everywhere on earth. It has been in large measure won in some countries, notably the United States.

The Catholic must fight totalitarianism of every kind that seeks to take away any of the fundamental or inalienable rights of man. Such rights are the right to life and to the integrity of the body, the right to marry and support a family in decency. These are natural rights, which go with man because he is man. But even rights that attach to man as citizen in a developed community can be called natural and inalienable, like the use of responsible freedom of expression—never to be confused with license. Pius XII upheld this right before the Third International Catholic Press Congress, February 18, 1950, in the words: "To reduce citizens to a forced silence is, in the eyes of every Christian, an outrage against the natural right of man, a violation of the order of the world as it was willed by God."

Does Catholicity Favor a World State?

Catholicity by its very nature can never favor the erasing of distinctive national characteristics, which help man to develop his personality. That is forbidden by the virtue of piety. It is the very purpose of Catholicity to reconcile the whole with its parts, as well as conversely.

But an international community of nations already exists by natural law, and Catholicity, by virtue of its principles, must equally work towards some form of effective world organization that will stop war. No other sovereigns in history have had such a long record of both statement and action in behalf of peace and international arbitration as have the Sovereign Pontiffs. Unity under an effective international organization, whereby every state must relinquish a part of its sovereignty for world peace, while retaining its "relative sovereignty," was a high point of Pius XII's Christmas Eve message of 1944. All these Christmas Eve messages, observed since 1939, have had peace and international organization in some aspect as their chief theme.

Since some form of international jurisdiction is essential for assured peace, Catholics cannot be indifferent to its establishment, though certainly no Catholic need underwrite the actions of the UN or the policies of the World Federalists.

Catholics cannot approve any comity of nations that denies to some the right to live. It is a fundamental Catholic teaching that the wealth of the world is for all, and that individual nations, like individual men, are only its stewards. This would preclude unreasonable tariffs, such as would paralyze world trade, and above all it demands reasonable world migration legislation. Pius XII made this especially clear in an address of October 18, 1951: "We do not need to say that the Catholic Church feels herself in the highest degree obliged to interest herself in migration questions. The relief of a great need is at stake. Lack of room and lack of means of existence makes this imperative."

The Common Good, the Great Regulator
of Catholic Policy

Catholicity is the religion par excellence of law, and law is defined as "an ordinance of reason for the common good." Not even God, insofar as He must obtain the ends for which He created men, can neglect the common good, for He is the Supreme Lawgiver. The common good cannot be understood in any utilitarian sense of the greatest material good of the greatest number. It refers to whatever, on balance, most advances the welfare of man as a child of God. Thus the revelation of a secret in Confession, though it might advance the temporal good of the community, would not be for the common good, since it would eventually redound to the odium of the sacrament of Penance, to the great spiritual loss of mankind.

It is this concern for the common good that explains why Catholicity can never be intolerant. Pius XII, in his historic address December 6, 1953, to the Italian jurists, but repeated the principles laid down by St. Thomas Aquinas and by St. Augustine and many another before him, when he said that which does not objectively correspond to truth or to the norm of morality has no right to exist or to be spread. "But, failure to impede this with civil laws and coercive measures can nevertheless be justified in the interests of a higher and more general good. . . . The duty of repressing moral and religious error cannot therefore be an ultimate norm of action. It must be subordinate to higher and more general norms, which in some circumstances permit, and even perhaps seem to indicate as the better policy, toleration of error in order to promote a greater good."

This is a simple restatement of Aquinas in the thirteenth century, who answered that unbelievers should be tolerated on account of some good that might arise or some evil that might be avoided, among which evils were "scandal, or the disturbance that might ensure, or some hindrance to the salvation of those who, were they unmolested, might gradually be converted to the Faith. For this reason the Church, at times, has tolerated the rites even of heretics and pagans, when unbelievers were very numerous." (*Summa,* Ia-IIae, q. 10, art. viii)

These words include every justification for tolerance that could conceivably be advanced. They explain why Catholic mission methods have been generally marked by forbearance as regards non-Christian religions, even among the Mohammedans of the age of the Crusades. (cf. *Osservatore Romano,* Jan. 8–9, 1955, *Le Missioni tra i Popoli Musulmani nel Sec. XIII*) They explain why Catholics were the first to introduce religious freedom into what is now the United States. "Hopital and Lord Baltimore," writes the rationalist William Lecky, a sharp critic of the Church, ". . . were the first two legislators who uniformly upheld religious liberty when in power; and Maryland continued the solitary refuge for the oppressed of every Christian sect. . . ." (*Rise of Rationalism in Europe,* II, p. 59)

For the United States, the final word about the Catholic attitude toward toleration can be taken from those uttered by the most renowned of American moral theologians, Father Francis Connell, C.SS.R., dean of the department of moral theology in the Catholic University: "Catholics should not hesitate to state that, even if at some future time the number of Catholics in the United States should become so great that they would possess the balance of voting power, there is no reason to believe that they would demand any special governmental favor for the Catholic Church or restrict the freedom of other religious groups. For it would still remain true that the evil consequences of any change of our traditional system of full freedom for all would far outweigh the benefits, so that the Catholics in such a hypothetical—though improbable—eventuality would be acting fully within the norms laid down by their Church if they continued the American tradition of equal rights for all religions." ("The Relationship Between Church and State," reprinted from *The Jurist,* Oct., 1953, p. 17)

The neutralist policy toward religions, though it will always be maintained, even by an overwhelmingly Catholic people, is not the absolute ideal in Catholic Church-State relations. Leo XIII said as much in his letter, *Longinqua Oceani,* to the Bishops of the United States: "The Church among you is hampered by no legal bonds, is protected against violence by common law and just judgments, and receives the opportunity to live and to act without being mistreated. But, although all this is true, it would be erroneous to conclude that from America is to be sought the example of the best condition of the Church, or that it is universally lawful and expedient for civil and religious matters to be dissociated, as in America. That Catholicism is in good condition among you, and is even enjoying a prosperous growth, is by all means to be ascribed to the fruitfulness of the Church, who, if she meets no adversary or hindrance, fructifies and expands of herself; but she would bring forth far more abundant fruits if, in addition to liberty, she enjoyed the favor of the laws and the patronage of public authority." (*Acta Leonis XIII,* vol. xvi, p. 7)

On What Is the Catholic Doctrine of Church-State Relationships Based?

Pius XI made this clear in his encyclical, *Quas Primas,* issued December 11, 1925: "Hence it follows, not only that Christ is to be adored as God by angels and men, but also that angels and men are to be obedient and subject to His rule as man. . . . He would grievously err who would deny to Christ the government of all civil matters, since He receives from the Father the most absolute right over created things."

Christ has communicated some measure of this power of His to the Church. By enjoining her to preach the Gospel everywhere (Matt. xxviii, 19; Mark xvi, 15), He gave her the right to plant missions everywhere, without hindrance. Of divine and not merely of natural right is the Church's claim to have her property exempt from taxation, and her clergy exempt from military service, and the right to establish marriage impediments for all baptized persons. The state, however, is independent of the Church in everything that has to do with its proper end, that is, matters purely temporal.

Pius XII declared to the Italian jurists (*op. cit.*): "In principle, that is, in theory, she [the Church] cannot approve complete separation of the two powers [Church and state]."

Leo XIII, in *Immortale Dei,* gives the reason for this: "Men joined in society are no less under the power of God than are individuals; and society owes no less gratitude to God than do individuals. . . . Hence, just as no one may neglect his duties to God, and just as it is the most important duty to embrace religion in soul and in conduct—not any religion one may choose but that which God has commanded and which is proved by certain and indubitable marks to be the only true religion of all religions—so too states may not without sin act as if God did not exist, or reject religion as irrelevant and unprofitable, or choose indifferently from all kinds of religions whichever they please, but they must, in worshiping the Divinity, employ that manner and mode in which God Himself has shown He wills to be worshiped."

Conclusion

ANY EXPOSITION of the Catholic Church must at the last paraphrase the celebrated sentence of Webster in his reply to Hayne: The Church—there she stands! The Church is an existential reality that does not fit into any genus or species. Catholicity is the religion of the whole, a religion in perfect accord with man in all his variety as well as his unity. Catholicity alone perfectly explains man to himself. It has always had its irrefutable answer to all attacks made upon it. Its claims can be obscured only by an appeal to what is not true or is misunderstood, or is at least irrelevant.

The Church survives the civilizations that she informs, though each of these earthly cities that succeed each other one by one find in her the source of their strength.

This singular fact that lies across all history will never perish, but will never attain here below an absolute and definitive triumph. From the beginning it has been, and until the end it will be, militant and opposed. It will never exhaust the work of testimony and evangelization that has been confided to it. It is as simple and as unfathomable as God Speaking.

Bibliography

DOGMATIC THEOLOGY

Bover, Maria José, *La asunción de Maria*. Madrid, 1947.
Diekamp, Francis, *Theologiae Dogmaticae Manuale*, 4 volumes. Paris, 1943.
Herve, J. M., *Manuale Theologicae Dogmaticae*, 4 volumes. Paris, 1935.
Hugon, Edouard, *Tractatus Dogmatici*, 4 volumes. Paris, 1927.
Lercher, Ludwig, *Institutiones Theologicae Dogmaticae*, 4 volumes. Innsbruck, 1924.
Tanquerey, Adolphe, *Brevior Synopsis Theologiae Dogmaticae*. Paris, 1913.

WORKS OF ST. THOMAS AQUINAS

Summa Contra Gentiles, Leonine edition. Paris, 1934.
Summa Theologica, 3 volumes, Dominican translation. New York, 1947.
Synopsis Totius Summae Theologicae S. Thomae, 3 volumes, abridged by Gerhardt Paris. Naples, 1950.

MORAL THEOLOGY

Aertnys, J. Damen, *Theologia Moralis*, 2 volumes. Rome, 1944.
Arregui, Antonio, *Summarium Theologiae Moralis*. Westminster, Md., 1944.
Connell, Francis J., *Outlines of Moral Theology*. Milwaukee, 1953.
————, *The Relationship Between Church and State*. Washington, D. C., 1954.
Genicot, E. Salsmans, *Institutiones Theologiae Moralis*, 2 volumes. Brussels, 1946.
Jone, Herbert, *Moral Theology*. Westminster, Md., 1948.
Merkelbach, Benedict, *Summa Theologiae Moralis*, 3 volumes. Paris, 1942.
Noldin, H. Schmitt, *Summa Theologiae Moralis*, 3 volumes. Innsbruck, 1941.
Ottaviani, Cardinal Alaphridus, *Compendium Iuris Publici Ecclesiastici*. Vatican City, 1936.
Pruemmer, M., *Manuale Theologiae Moralis*. Barcelona, 1945.
Sabetti, Aloysius Barrett, *Compendium Theologiae Moralis*. New York, 1939.
Tanquerey, Adolphe, *Synopsis Theologiae Moralis*. New York, 1904.
Vermeersch, Arthur, *Theologiae Moralis*, 3 volumes. Rome, 1948.

COMPILATIONS AND ENCYCLOPEDIAS

Catholic Almanac. Paterson, N. J., 1955.

Catholic Encyclopedia, 15 volumes. New York, 1912.

Dictionary of Dogmatic Theology, edited by Pietro Parente. Milwaukee, 1951.

Dictionnaire apologétique de la foi catholique, 4 volumes. Paris, 1928.

Dictionnaire de la théologie catholique, 15 volumes. Paris, 1952.

Enciclopedia Apologetica, Italian translation of *Apologétique.* Rome, 1954.

Herders Sozial-Katechismus, 2 volumes. Freiburg, Germany, 1951, 1952.

PHILOSOPHY

Cathrein, Victor, *Philosophia Moralis.* Barcelona, 1945.

Farges, Albert Barbedette, *Philosophia Scholastica,* 2 volumes. Paris, 1931.

Rommen, Heinrich, *Natural Law.* St. Louis, 1947.

———, *The State in Catholic Thought.* St. Louis, 1947.

Sertillanges, A., *Les grandes thèses de la philosophie thomiste,* Paris, 1928.

DOGMATIC AND CHURCH HISTORY

Ante-Nicene Fathers, compiled by A. Cleveland Coxe, Volumes I and II. New York, 1885.

Balmes, Jaime, *El protestantismo comparado con el catolicismo.* Madrid, 1949.

Denziger, Henricus, *Enchiridion Symbolorum.* St. Louis, 1936.

De Journel, Rouet, *Enchiridion Patristicum.* Barcelona, 1946.

Guilday, Peter, *The Life and Times of John Carroll.* New York, 1922.

Harnack, Adolf, *What Is Christianity?* New York, 1901.

Iglesias, Eduardo, *El Reino.* Mexico City, 1950.

Kirch, Conrad, *Enchiridion Fontium Historiae Ecclesiasticae Antiquae.* Barcelona, 1947.

Lake, Kirsopp, *Apostolic Fathers,* Volume I. London, 1925.

Latourette, Kenneth, *History of Christian Missions in China.* New York, 1929.

Lecky, William, *Rise of Rationalism in Europe.* New York 1910.

Lunn, Arnold Coulton, *Is the Catholic Church Anti-Social?* London, 1947.

McSorley, Joseph, *Outline History of the Church by Centuries.* St. Louis, 1950.

Newman, John Henry Cardinal, *Essay on the Development of Christian Doctrine.* New York, 1845.

———, *Idea of a University.* London, 1873.

Walsh, James, *Thirteenth, Greatest of Centuries.* New York, 1907.

Wayman, Dorothy G., *Cardinal O'Connell of Boston*. New York, 1955.

Young, Alfred, *Catholic and Protestant Countries Compared*. New York, 1895.

CATECHISMS AND POPULAR EXPLANATIONS

Catechismus Catholicus, edited by Pietro Cardinal Gasparri. Vatican City, 1930.

Ciarlantini, Lino, *The Liberty of the School and Family Education*. New York, 1954.

Conway, Bertrand, *Question Box*. New York, 1929.

Deharb, Joseph, *Complete Catechism of the Catholic Religion*. New York, 1908.

Gibbons, James Cardinal, *Faith of Our Fathers*. New York, 1895.

Graham, Henry G., *Where We Got the Bible*. St. Louis, 1952.

Sullivan, John F. (rev. by O'Leary), *The Externals of the Catholic Church*. New York, 1951.

This We Believe, Baltimore Catechism No. 3, revised. Paterson, N. J., 1954.

Trese, Leo, *God, Man, and God-Man*. Paterson, N. J., 1954.

CANON LAW

Brown, M. J., *The Catholic Matrimonial Courts*. New York, 1928.

Woywood, Stanislas, *A Practical Commentary on the Code of Canon Law*, 2 volumes. New York, 1929.

ENCYCLICALS AND ALLOCUTIONS

Leo XIII, *Rerum Novarum*. Five Great Encyclicals. New York, 1955.

Pius XI, *Casti Connubii, Christian Education of Youth, Quadragesimo Anno*. Five Great Encyclicals. New York, 1939.

Pius XII, *Humani Generis*. New York, 1951.

———, *The Mystical Body of Christ*. New York, 1943.

———, *The World Community*, translation of *Ci Riesci*, delivered December 6, 1953. New York, 1954.

PERIODICALS

America (New York), 1954.

American Ecclesiastical Review (Washington, D. C.), 1954.

Catholic Herald (London), 1954.

Civilta Cattolica (Rome), 1950–1954.

La Croix (Paris), 1950–1954.

Herder-Korrespondenz (Freiburg, Germany), 1953–1954.

Latinoamerica (Mexico City), 1949–1954.

Osservatore Romano (Vatican City), 1950–1954.

Tablet (London), 1949–1954.

About the Author

PAUL H. HALLETT, literary and associate editor of *The Register,* a Catholic newspaper with the largest circulation of any religious newspaper in the world, comes in daily contact with the questions commonly asked of *The Register* by both Catholics and non-Catholics about Catholic doctrine and practice. He edits six columns for *The Register,* the best-known of which is "Keeping Up with Events." Born in Colorado, he became a convert to Catholicity at the age of twenty. He was graduated from Regis College in Denver with the Poetry, Literature, History, and Latin prizes. By himself he acquired a knowledge of Greek, Hebrew, and four other languages. He has translated twelve of the Latin theological texts generally used in Catholic seminaries—among them Herve's *Manuale Theologicae Dogmaticae,* Tanquerey's *Brevior,* and Paris' condensation of the *Summa*—for the use of the Register College of Journalism. For *What Is Catholicity?* he has drawn heavily upon long study of the great theologians of the past, especially St. Thomas, and those of the present day. He lives in Denver, Colorado, where *The Register* is published.